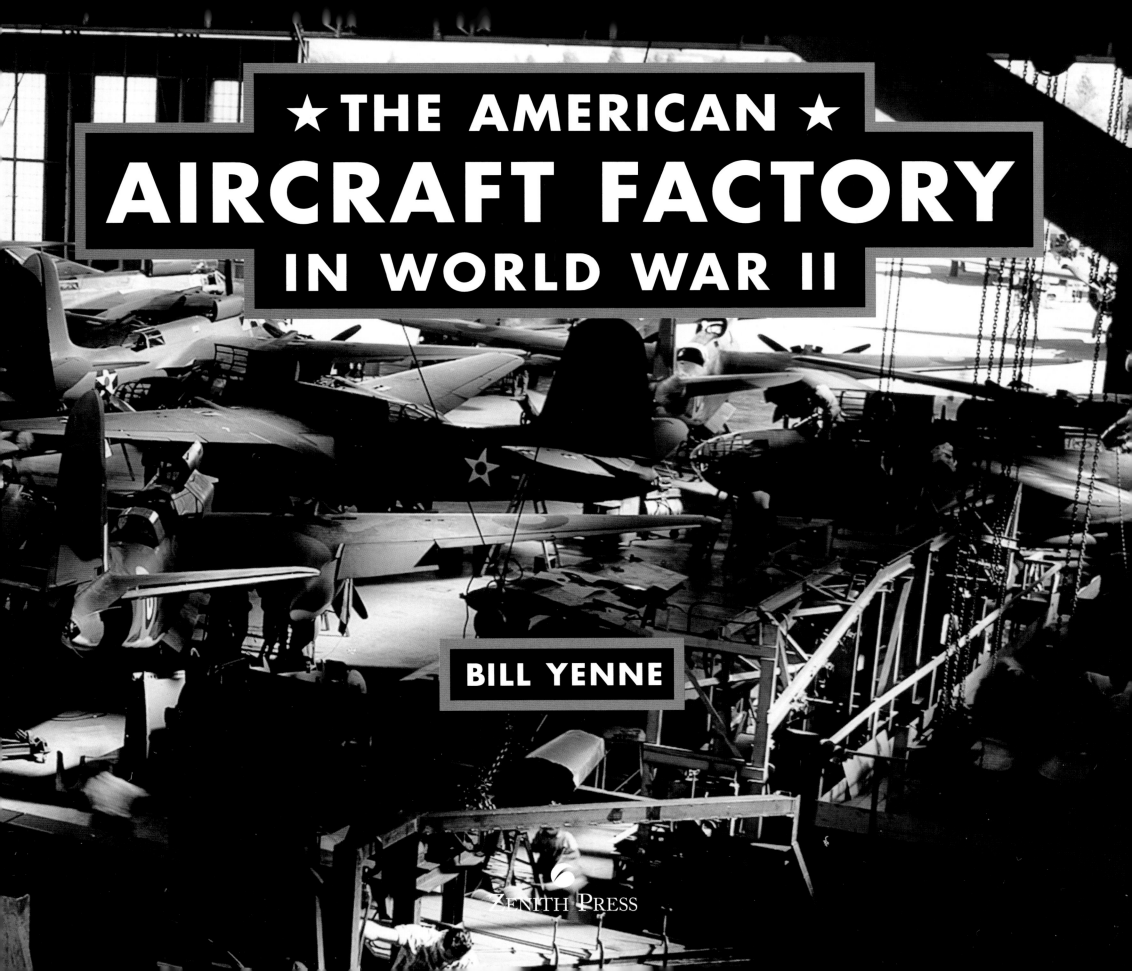

★ THE AMERICAN ★
AIRCRAFT FACTORY
IN WORLD WAR II

BILL YENNE

ZENITH PRESS

First published in 2006 by MBI Publishing Company LLC and Zenith Press, an imprint of MBI Publishing Company, Galtier Plaza, Suite 200, 380 Jackson Street, St Paul, MN, 55101-3885 USA

Zenith Press books are also available at discounts in bulk quantity for industrial or sales-promotional use. For details write to Special Sales Manager at MBI Wholesalers & Distributors, Galtier Plaza, Suite 200, 380 Jackson Street, St Paul, MN, 55101-3885 USA.

Library of Congress Cataloging-in-Publication Data

Yenne, Bill, 1949-
    The American aircraft factory in World War II / Bill Yenne.
      p. cm.
    Includes index.
    ISBN-13: 978-0-7603-2300-7 (hardcover with jacket)
    ISBN-10: 0-7603-2300-3 (hardcover with jacket)
  1. Airplane factories—United States—Pictorial works. 2. Airplane factories—United States—History--20th century—Sources. 3. World War, 1939-1945—Equipment and supplies—Pictorial works. 4. Industrial mobilization—United States—History—20th century—Sources. I. Title.
    TL724.Y46 2006
    623.74'6097309044—dc22

                                                                 2006010917

Editor: Dennis Pernu
Designer: Christopher Fayers

Printed in China

Front cover: The term "Arsenal of Democracy," coined during World War II to describe American industry, was certainly evident in this picture of B-17G Flying Fortresses taking shape on the Boeing factory floor. The term is also applicable when one notes that American aircraft factories not only provided about 300,000 airplanes to American forces, but nearly 40,000 to the British Commonwealth as well. In just a few years, the American aircraft factory grew from a negligible portion of the American economy to the number one American industry. *Boeing Archives*

Endpapers: Seeing nearly two dozen forward fuselages for B-17 Flying Fortresses on the floor at one time gives a true sense of the term "Arsenal of Democracy." *Boeing Archives*

Frontispiece: Douglas technicians conduct the precise installation of a Pratt & Whitney R1830 Twin Wasp radial engine in a C-47 at the Long Beach plant. *Alfred Palmer, Office of War Information*

Title pages: An overview of the factory floor at the Douglas Aircraft Company's flagship plant in Santa Monica, probably taken in 1941 on the eve of the United States' entry into the war. Most of the aircraft seen here are the durable attack bombers that were delivered to Britain's Royal Air Force as the Boston and to the USAAF as the A-20 Havoc. On the left is the massive tail of the XB-19, an experimental, one-of-a-kind super-bomber that first flew in 1941 but was not placed into production. *Courtesy Harry Gann*

Back cover: Technician Norma Janson stands amid the abstract pattern formed by this forest of completed B-29 Superfortress tail sections on the floor at Boeing's Renton facility. *Boeing Archives*

The production totals and dollar figures given throughout this book are derived from official corporate or military data. Production totals vary and may be different than data from other sources because of different interpretations of beginning and ending dates used to compile the data. Manufacturers usually include all production regardless of when it began or ended. Official government records of quantities and dollars typically begin with July 1940, December 1941, or a date in between. This same data may end at any point between August and December 1945. Foreign data is often reckoned from 1938 or 1939. Rounding off for a given month or year by one source may shift data from one month forward or backward to the adjacent month, placing it at a variance with another source that shifted it another way. Meanwhile, some sources count completions and other sources count deliveries, leading to separate numbers that don't necessarily agree. Therefore, totals should be considered approximate to within a reasonable margin. Current dollar conversions are estimates based on current values at press time and should be considered valuable as general estimates for the sake of comparison only.

CONTENTS

Acknowledgments

I wish to thank Mike Lombardi and Tom Lubbesmeyer of the Boeing Archives, as well as Eric Schulzinger of Lockheed, Erik Simonsen of Boeing, Earl Blount of North American Aviation, and the late, great Harry Gann of Douglas for many years of assistance in my research and writing about American aircraft manufacturers.

Crowded cheek by jowl in Shop 308 at Boeing's Plant 2 in Seattle, these aft fuselage/tail sections will all be gone within a week, having been incorporated into B-17 Flying Fortresses. *Boeing Archives*

The "Arsenal of Democracy" is seen in action as a progression of Douglas C-47A-75-DL Skytrains move down the line at Long Beach. The sign tells us that the line will move at ten minutes past five, but that could be either morning or afternoon—during World War II, the American aircraft factory generally operated 24 hours a day. *Courtesy Harry Gann*

Introduction

During World War II, the United States became the largest producer of aircraft that the world has ever seen, or will almost certainly ever see again. On the eve of the war, the American aircraft factory was a quaint job shop, where aircraft were virtually handmade by the craft method abandoned by the American automobile factory a generation before. Within just a few years, it would be transformed into the largest single industry in the world. Among American industries, the aviation industry rose to first place from forty-first place.

Prior to World War II, the American aircraft industry ranked fifth in the world, but during the war it became the global leader, producing twice as many aircraft as the United Kingdom or the Soviet Union, and 1.6 times as many aircraft as the three major Axis powers—Germany, Italy, and Japan—combined. According to the Civil Aeronautic Administration *Statistical Handbook*, America's aircraft factories produced 324,750 aircraft between 1939 and 1945, including 304,139 military aircraft. The rate of increase in the output of the American aircraft industry is hard to comprehend: in 1939, a total of 921 military aircraft were built in the United States. In 1944, the industry reached a peak annual production of 96,318.

The American aircraft industry produced 158,880 aircraft for the U.S. Army Air Forces, America's principal air arm, and 73,711 aircraft for the U.S. Navy. American industry alone built 38,811 for the British Commonwealth air forces from 1940, while British industry itself produced just 131,549 from 1939.

In the pages that follow, I will trace the details behind these astounding statistics and examine the inner workings of a remarkable industry at its greatest moment.

The American aircraft industry was and is composed of four relatively distinct groups. First and foremost are the airframe manufacturers, which were and are the largest component of the industry in terms of employment, dollar volume, and the sheer weight of their output. Second are the engine manufacturers, which were and are responsible for the single most complex component of any powered aircraft. Third are the subcontractors that provide subassemblies and components. Finally, there are the vendors of accessories and small parts from rivets and cables to turrets and shock absorbers.

During World War II, the largest airframe manufacturers in the American aircraft industry were Bell, Boeing, Consolidated-Vultee, Curtiss (a component of Curtiss-Wright), Douglas, Grumman, Lockheed, Martin, North American Aviation, and Republic. Each of these companies and its major products are discussed in detail in the pages that follow. The major makers of radial aircraft engines were Wright Aeronautical, a division of Curtiss-Wright, and Pratt & Whitney, a division of United Aircraft. The largest makers of inline aircraft engines were the Allison Division of General Motors and the Packard Motor Company.

Beginning with the origins of America's great aviation pioneers and the companies they created, this book examines the remarkable evolution of the American aircraft industry during World War II and tells the story of the American aircraft factory's metamorphosis from a relic of a fading industrial era to the technological leader among American industries.

This photo of a typical "Rosie the Riveter" captures the amazing enthusiasm and vitality of the American workforce during World War II. Women entered that workforce in record numbers during the war, and in no major industry were they better paid than in the aircraft sector. *Courtesy Harry Gann*

Chapter One

America's First Planemakers

During World War II, the American aircraft industry reached levels of production and technology that would have been unthinkable four decades earlier—within the adult lifetimes of many people who were alive during the war. In four decades, aviation had come from nowhere. Occurring a few years after the century began, the advent of powered, fixed-wing flight would help frame the technological, cultural, and military history of the twentieth century. It might have happened anywhere in the world, but it happened in America.

The way that it happened played out like a Hollywood movie, the kind of triumph-over-adversity film that Americans love. In this story, a pair of underfinanced underdogs working in a bicycle shop in a wholesome little Midwestern town faced off against the well-financed efforts of a proud, well-educated, and overconfident Bostonian with financial backing from the establishment.

The underdogs won.

America's first aircraft factory was a bike shop!

In the fall of 1903, if a wagering person had been called to bet upon who would first achieve manned heavier-than-air flight, that person would have wagered on Samuel Pierpont Langley. Langley had the technical background and the virtually unlimited support of the Smithsonian Institution and the U.S. War Department. And he had an aircraft that was almost ready to fly—almost.

Langley had studied engineering in Boston and Chicago and held the chair in astronomy at Western University of Pennsylvania (later the University of Pittsburgh) from 1867 to 1886. In 1887, he was appointed secretary of the Smithsonian Institution in Washington, D.C., where he established the Astrophysical Observatory.

Langley had also become interested in aviation and obsessed with the notion of heavier-than-air flight. In 1896, he successfully flew a 25-pound model airplane, named *Aerodrome No. 5* and powered by a single-horsepower steam engine. This test, done in the presence of government officials and such notables as Alexander Graham Bell, inspired a great deal of official interest—and funding.

The *Aerodrome A*, as Langley dubbed his first piloted machine, was completed and ready for flight-testing in the autumn of 1903. Langley's plan was to launch the *Aerodrome A* from a catapult constructed on the

The Wright brothers beat him into the air, but Glenn Hammond Curtiss became America's first successful planemaker. Dozens of JN-4s line the floor at the Curtiss Aeroplane & Motor Company Bristol Fuselage plant on July 20, 1918, at the apogee of the World War I airplane boom. *Author collection*

RIGHT: Glenn Luther Martin starred opposite Mary Pickford in the 1915 silent film *Girl of Yesterday*. Martin earned $700 a day (approximately $13,500 in current dollars) to fly his Model TT biplane in the film. *Author collection*

OPPOSITE: Glenn Curtiss shows off one of his early "hydroaeroplanes" to Henry Ford at Keuka Lake, near Hammondsport, New York. *Author collection*

roof of a houseboat anchored in the Potomac River. On October 7, everyone held their breath as the *Aerodrome A* shot forward on the catapult—and everyone gasped as it crashed into the river. Langley and his large competent Smithsonian/War Department crew rebuilt the *Aerodrome A* and went about preparations to try again. The date was set for December 8. This time, the rear wing failed on launch and the disintegrating craft fell into the Potomac, temporarily trapping the pilot, who also happened to be Langley's assistant, Charles M. Manly, in the cold, dark waters. Manly was once again rescued unhurt, and Langley issued an official statement that the project was over.

On December 17, 1903, less than two weeks after the great Samuel Pierpont Langley gave up in disgust, two young tinkerers from Dayton, Ohio, achieved mankind's age-old dream on a windswept sand dune at Kill Devil Hills near Kitty Hawk, North Carolina. Wilbur and Orville Wright realized the goal of powered human flight in a heavier-than-air vehicle.

The brothers made numerous demonstration flights in the United States and traveled to Europe in 1908, where the French, who had accused them of bluffing, were greatly impressed. In the countries where the governments had turned down military versions of the *Wright Flyer*, there was now interest from private parties and the Wrights issued licenses for firms in Britain, France, and Germany to build their aircraft.

By 1909, however, only six short years after the triumph at Kill Devil Hills, the tide was running out for the brothers. For centuries, humans had dreamed of flight but were unable to construct the

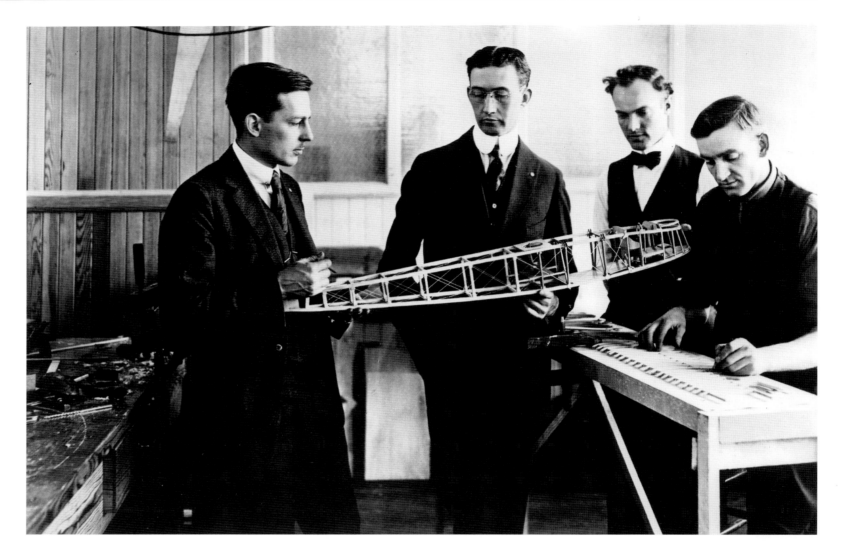

Glenn Martin (center) inspects a scale model of the Glenn Martin Bomber (GMB) at his Cleveland, Ohio, factory around New Year's in 1917. The airplane was actually designed by Donald Wills Douglas (left). Men identified as H. Carr and Ross Elkins are on the right. *Courtesy Harry Gann*

machine to make it possible. But now that the aviation genie was out of the bottle; they had numerous competitors. The Wright brothers had created an invention that would revolutionize the course of world history, but they had failed to create a business enterprise to exploit their invention and to achieve financial success proportional to their technological success. The Wrights were aeronautical geniuses, but they were not entrepreneurs.

Glenn Hammond Curtiss possessed the proclivity for self-promotion that the Wrights lacked. He built and flew his first airplane in 1908 and never looked back. In 1916, Curtiss, along with investment banker Clement Melville Keys and John North Willys of the Willys-Overland Motor Company, formed the publicly traded Curtiss Aeroplane & Motor Company, Inc., to consolidate Curtiss aircraft, engineering, and engine-manufacturing activities. Keys would help Glenn Curtiss transform America's first *successful* airplane company.

Less than a year later, the United States entered World War I and, thanks to Keys, the Curtiss Aeroplane & Motor Company was structured in such a way as to be able to quickly develop the production capacity to take maximum advantage of the military's sudden, voracious appetite for aircraft and engines.

After the Wrights and Curtiss, a third name that entered the pantheon of America's first generation of great planemakers was that of Glenn Luther Martin, who taught himself to fly in 1909, using a pusher biplane that he designed and built himself. Martin formed his own company and divided his time between exhibition flying and designing aircraft, and in 1912 he set up his first factory in Santa Ana. After a few years in California, he merged briefly with Orville Wright in 1916 to form the short-lived Wright-Martin Aircraft Company. A year later, Martin left to form a second Glenn L. Martin Company based in Cleveland, Ohio, and Wright-Martin dissolved. During the

Donald Douglas and his crew hand-built the Davis-Douglas Cloudster in 1920 and 1921. David Davis left the airplane business after just this one aircraft, but Don Douglas stayed, building his company into one of America's largest. That's him inside the fuselage at the far right. *Courtesy Harry Gann*

war, Martin received the order for the Army's first twin-engine bomber under the simple designation GMB (for "Glenn Martin Bomber"). The GMB was first flown on August 15, 1918, but the war ended three months later before it could be used in combat. However, it set the stage for large-aircraft development in the United States.

World War I was the first aviation war, but the American aircraft moved sluggishly and barely made it into the game. World War I found the fledgling factories utterly unprepared to be anything but bit players in the huge drama of the world's first great aircraft boom. Though airplanes had been invented in the United States, other countries, mainly France, Germany, and Britain, quickly became world leaders in aviation technology and production.

Glenn Curtiss was notable for having developed and built the most widely produced American design of the World War I era. Known familiarly as the "Jenny," the Curtiss JN series (especially the JN-4) was produced in larger numbers than any other American airplane of the 1914–1918 period or before. Nearly 8,500 JN-4s were built, and they were used mainly as trainers.

The greatest contribution to military aviation by American factories in World War I was not an airframe but an engine. Designed by Jesse Vincent and E. J. Hall of the Hall-Scott Motor Company, the Liberty L12 was a V-12 water cooled, 1,650-ci overhead-cam engine delivering 400 horsepower. However, this contribution did not come from the American aircraft industry but from the American automobile industry. Working under license, United States automakers (including Ford, General Motors, Lincoln, Marmon, Nordyke, and Packard) manufactured 20,478 Liberties in the nearly two years beginning on July 4, 1917. Manufacturing by multiple factories run by multiple companies was facilitated by a modular design in which four or six cylinders could be used in one or two banks. Hall-Scott

This was the Douglas Aircraft Company machine shop in about 1921. Not only was every moving part handmade, many parts were engineered on the workbench. *Courtesy Harry Gann*

This aerial view shows the Douglas Aircraft Company factory, a former movie studio, on Wilshire Boulevard in Santa Monica as it appeared in 1922. An O-2 observation plane for the U.S. Army is on the right. *Courtesy Harry Gann*

engines would continue to be common in American aircraft through the 1920s.

The story of the Liberty engine illustrates dramatically how much more developed the automobile industry was in 1917. In the 1920s, the United States aircraft industry would just begin to hit its stride.

The 1920s would see modest growth in the American aircraft industry, although nothing like that experienced in the automobile industry. The prosperity of the Roaring Twenties unleashed a great deal of demand for cars, but the planemakers competed with a huge number of barely used World War I surplus aircraft. For sport pilots and individual users there were plenty of Curtiss Jennies that were sturdy and reliable, and available more cheaply than were new airplanes. However, the growing number of airlines and the military were interested in new technology: larger aircraft and aircraft with better performance in terms of speed, range, and service ceiling.

During the 1920s, the aviation industry went from wood-and-fabric biplanes held together by wire, to large all-metal, multiengine monoplanes with sound-proofed passenger cabins and the ability to cruise comfortably at altitudes that would have intimidated pilots in 1919. The war years had seen a refinement in the reliability and performance of airframes and an improvement in "aero engine" technology. The sputtering four-cylinder engines of the early days were replaced by thundering V-8s.

In the late 1920s, the civilian market represented a much larger portion of the aircraft market than did the military. In 1928, the armed forces acquired only 1,219 of the 4,346 new aircraft sold in the United States. During the Great Depression the two evened out, but in 1936, the civilian market rebounded, buying 1,559 new aircraft to the military's 1,141.

Many of the most important "aeronautical" manufacturing companies of the twentieth century took root on the West Coast far from America's industrial heartland. American industry originated in the Northeast and the Great Lakes country. Those regions were population centers and transportation hubs and were close to essential raw materials:

A guard challenges a caller at the Boeing Company's "Red Barn" factory in June 1917. The United States was in World War I and Boeing was doing war work. William Edward Boeing built his first airplane in his boathouse on Lake Union in the heart of Seattle in 1916, but soon moved to this location south of downtown. Eventually, the vast Boeing Field complex grew outward from here. The Red Barn still exists and is part of the Museum of Flight. *Boeing Archives*

iron and coal. The aircraft industry moved west for an essential natural resource that cities in the Northeast and the Great Lakes region couldn't offer: excellent year-round flying weather.

Glenn Martin pioneered the industry's move westward. Though Glenn Martin returned east, other aircraft manufacturers went west to stay. Still others were born in the West. A case in point: one of the key engineers on Martin's 1918 GMB project was a young man whose name would become one of the biggest in American aviation, almost synonymous with California planemaking in the twentieth century—Donald Wills Douglas.

Don Douglas, who became one of the leading captains of California industry for several decades, was born in Brooklyn, New York, and graduated from the Massachusetts Institute of Technology (MIT) two years ahead of schedule in 1914. A year later, he was hired by Glenn Martin. In 1920, Douglas decided to strike out on his own with the backing of David R. Davis, a well-heeled young financier who was intrigued with the idea of undertaking the difficult task of flying coast to coast nonstop. Douglas accepted the challenge and hired some former colleagues from Martin to help design and build what turned out to be a beautiful plane that he called the Cloudster.

After the Cloudster failed to become the first plane to fly coast to coast nonstop, Davis lost interest in the joint venture, but Douglas did not. Even before Davis made his exit from one side of the stage, the U.S. Navy made its entrance from the opposite side with orders for airplanes. It was the beginning of a long relationship.

In 1924, under a U.S. Army contract, Douglas' company built the Douglas World Cruisers, the first aircraft to completely circumnavigate the world. The 25,553 miles took six months. Although the Cloudster had failed to become the first airplane to fly coast to coast nonstop, only three years later Douglas had built the first planes to fly around the world. The image of three airplanes circling the globe became the Douglas logo.

Up the coast in San Francisco, they still talk about that foggy June morning in 1913 when Allan and Malcolm Loughead trucked their Model G floatplane down to the foot of Laguna Street. Allan climbed into the cockpit, coaxed the 80-horsepower Curtiss V8 engine to life, taxied across the cold waters of San Francisco Bay, and lifted the Model G into the air. Allan and Malcolm had shown a great deal of interest in things mechanical as they were growing up, and Allan had learned to fly on early Curtiss machines. Later, they were aided by their older half

An early Boeing pursuit plane is loaded for shipment to the U.S. Army in June 1922. *Boeing Archives*

brother, Victor Loughead, an aeronautical engineer by avocation, in developing their first air plane. The Model G was the first successful tractor seaplane (front mounted propeller) in the United States, and it came just two years after Glenn Curtiss pioneered America's first sea plane.

After making good money offering sightseeing excursions at the San Francisco Panama Pacific Exposition, the brothers moved south to Santa Barbara. There they tinkered with several designs, including their F-1 seaplane, before folding their company. By 1926, however, they were back on the scene, and the company with the phonetic pronunciation of their name—Lockheed—was back to stay.

Between the world wars, one of the most important names to show up on the staff roster at both the Lockheed and Douglas companies was that of John Knudsen Northrop. He designed the wings for the Loughead F-1 seaplane, but in 1923, after the collapse of the Loughead brothers' first company, Northrop was hired by Donald Douglas to work at his Santa Monica plant. After a few years with Douglas, Northrop moved back to the newly constituted Lockheed Company where he designed his first masterpiece, the Lockheed Vega. In 1928, Northrop moved again, this time to the little Avion Corporation in Burbank, California, a company where he hoped to try out some of his

own, more innovative designs. A year later, Avion became Northrop Aircraft Corporation, but it fell on hard times during the Great Depression. In 1932, Northrop reorganized, forming a new Northrop Corporation with Don Douglas owning a 51 percent share. The new company became a division of Douglas Aircraft in 1938, and Jack Northrop put together a syndicate of investors to start another new Northrop in 1939.

Up the coast in Seattle, Washington, another man whose name would come to be one of the greatest in American planemaking was also getting started in his career in the years preceding World War II. William Edward Boeing attended Yale University but left for the Northwest in 1903. After making his fortune in the timber industry near Gray's Harbor, Washington, Boeing moved to Seattle in 1908. There, he was involved in a variety of business ventures related to wood products, including a furniture factory and a boatyard. In 1910, he attended the first major American air show near Los Angeles and was bitten by the aviation bug. He and his friend George Conrad Westervelt, a naval officer and MIT-trained engineer stationed at the U.S. Navy shipyard in Bremerton, near Seattle, decided to build an airplane. As Westervelt worked up the design, Boeing went to California to take flying lessons from Glenn Martin.

RIGHT: William Edward Boeing (with hat, right) pays a visit to the factory, accompanied by Mrs. Boeing and company president Edgar Gott (with hat, center) in early 1922. The contraptions that look like sinks are actually cockpit bottoms.
Boeing Archives

OPPOSITE: "Rosie the Riveter" was not new to the American aircraft industry in World War II. Here, a group of women help assemble a Boeing FB-5 for the U.S. Navy in January 1927. Note the Packard 2A-1500 inline engine. Even before World War II, American automakers already had much experience building aircraft engines.
Boeing Archives

The first Boeing aircraft was built in Bill Boeing's boathouse on Lake Union in Seattle. The first flight came on June 15, 1916, with Bill Boeing himself at the controls. He taxied out across the smooth surface of Lake Union and lifted it into the air. A month after the first flight, Bill Boeing incorporated the Pacific Aero Products Company to build and market floatplanes. A year later, it became the Boeing Company. Boeing's early floatplanes were marketed both to commercial customers and to the U.S. Navy. The United States entered World War I less than a year after the Model 1's debut.

By the early 1920s, planemakers were popping up throughout the country. Clyde Cessna, Lloyd Stearman, and Walter Beech were all building airplanes in Wichita, Kansas. On the East Coast, there were a number of small aircraft companies started in the late teens and early 1920s. While many are long forgotten to all but a few aviation enthusiasts, they formed the building blocks of companies—or employed skilled engineers—that would become household names during World War II and remain important stars in the pantheon of great planemakers. Take, for example, Gallaudet Engineering Company, formed in 1908 in Norwich, Connecticut, by 31-year-old Edson Gallaudet. By 1922, the company was in financial trouble and its directors instructed general manager Reuben Hollis Fleet to shape things up and report back in 90 days. Fleet shaped things up: he recommended that the company be liquidated. Fleet told the directors that he would form his own company and offered to fulfill the Gallaudet contracts, paying the directors 10 percent of his own net worth to rent the former Gallaudet plant.

In 1923, Fleet formed the Consolidated Aircraft Corporation by consolidating several components, including Gallaudet and a portfolio of designs that he purchased from General Motors when they closed their Dayton-Wright subsidiary. In September 1924, having already achieved modest success, Fleet moved Consolidated to new facilities in Buffalo, New York, where there was a surplus of skilled labor that had been drawn to the factories of the Great Lakes port city during World War I. In Buffalo, Reuben Fleet began building flying boats. In 1928 Fleet and his general manager, Isaac Machlin "Mac" Laddon, developed the XPY-1 Admiral, which was billed as "the largest flying boat built in the United States." In 1933, Consolidated began delivering its new P2Y Ranger seaplane to the U.S. Navy. With Lake Erie frozen for part of the year, however, Fleet grew fed up trying to build flying boats in Buffalo, so in 1935 he abandoned the bitter Northeast winters for San Diego's mellow climate. There he established himself as another major player in the California aircraft industry.

Probably the greatest consolidator in the history of the American aviation industry was financier and investment banker Clement Melville Keys, a visionary who brought a number of important aviation pioneers together, however briefly, under the same corporate umbrella. As previously noted, in 1916, Keys and John North Willys of the Willys-Overland Motor Company, came together to form the Curtiss Aeroplane & Motor Company, propelling it into industry leadership. Keys was the man who helped Glenn Curtiss transform America's first successful airplane company. After the war, as the market for new airplanes lagged dramatically, Willys sold his shares to Keys, who became the largest shareholder in Curtiss. Though he never engineered an airplane, in August 1929—two months before the October stock market crash—Keys engineered the spectacular merger that brought together America's two pioneering aircraft builders—Curtiss and Wright—to form the Curtiss-Wright Corporation. In a final irony to the story of the rivalry between Glenn Curtiss and the Wright brothers, Keys brought the first two names in American aviation under one corporate roof. The founders, meanwhile, faded away. Wilbur Wright died in 1912, followed by Curtiss in 1930. Orville Wright had retired into obscurity though he lived until 1948.

Curtiss-Wright would have two principal divisions, the aircraft division in Buffalo, New York, that made airplanes with the Curtiss brand name, and the division that made engines in Ohio under the Wright brand name.

In the meantime, Keys laid out plans for another elaborate and complex holding company that would form a framework for his intended future plans. This holding company—North American Aviation, Inc.—was to be 70 percent–owned by Keys' own Curtiss Aeroplane & Motor Company, with 12 percent of the shares owned by each of two airlines: Transcontinental Air Transport (TAT) and the Curtiss Flying Service. Donald Douglas, that young airplane builder in California, bought into the company for the remaining 6 percent.

In 1929, Keys brought the Pitcairn Aviation Company (founded in 1925) and the Sperry Gyroscope Company (founded in 1910) into the North American Aviation fold. Pitcairn (started by Pittsburgh Plate Glass Pitcairns) also owned a fledgling airline, which had by then become Eastern Air Transport (and which would ultimately become Eastern Air Lines). In 1930, Keys acquired the Ford Instrument Company (formed in 1916), which, along with Berliner-Joyce Aircraft (formed in 1926), also became part of the North American Aviation "family" of companies. By 1934, the holding company owned 27.6 percent of TAT (its former parent) and 52 percent of Western Air Express (WAE). These companies would ultimately become Trans World Airlines (TWA) and Western Airlines, respectively.

In the meantime, other empire builders were taking the field. Henry Ford, America's greatest entrepreneur of the early twentieth century, had developed an excellent tri-motor airliner and was making noises about an airline company. General Motors, the world's largest corporation and Ford's most bitter rival in the automobile industry, moved to compete with Ford in aviation.

As with Clement Melville Keys, William C. Durant had grown his General Motors through acquisitions—Buick, Cadillac, and Oldsmobile in 1909 and Chevrolet after World War I. General Motors' opening move in the world of aviation was the May 1929 acquisition of 40 percent of Fokker Aircraft, the firm started by Tony Fokker. Known in the industry as the "Flying Dutchman," the Java-born Fokker had designed the best warplanes flown by Germany during World War I and had built the best air transports in the world in the early 1920s. Renamed as General Aviation Manufacturing Corporation in 1930, Fokker Aircraft was a true plum and formed the cornerstone of General Aviation Corporation (GAC), the holding company that General Motors formed as a parent company for aircraft interests.

In late 1933—through GAC—General Motors acquired a 30 percent share of North American Aviation and installed Ernest R. Breech as chairman of the board. The world's largest corporation now owned the remnants of three important early aircraft builders—Berliner-Joyce, Fokker, and Pitcairn—as well as the seedling airlines that ultimately evolved into Western Airlines, Eastern Air Lines, and TWA.

In 1934, the entire face of the U.S. commercial aviation industry was transformed when the newly elected Roosevelt administration pushed through the Airmail Act, which decreed (in part) that an airline could not own an airplane manufacturer or vice versa. General Motors theorized that this controversial piece of legislation did not cover a *third* company owning one of *each*. The industrial giant disposed of all of its holdings, except for Eastern Air Lines and North American Aviation, which were reconfigured as autonomous operating companies. General Motors would sell its interests in Eastern Air Lines in 1938 and in North American Aviation in 1948.

OPPOSITE: Things were very busy on the floor at the Boeing factory on June 3, 1927. In the foreground, Model 40A mail planes are taking shape, while PW-9 fighters, destined for the U.S. Army, can be seen in the background. Boeing was one of the first companies to use arc-welded steel instead of wood in its aircraft designs. *Boeing Archives*

This welder looks very dapper in his tie and vest. Even as late as the 1930s, many important parts for Consolidated aircraft were made meticulously by hand. Both the technology and the dress code would later change. *Author collection*

Unlike many early aircraft companies, North American Aviation was directed with the passion of an entrepreneur, rather than the calculation of an engineer, by the man who was present at its birth: Clement Melville Keys. By the time the North American Aviation appellation was attached to a newly developed aircraft, Keys had moved on, and a new man—James Howard "Dutch" Kindelberger—had emerged to guide the company through its defining years.

Technically, North American Aviation was founded in 1928, but it was really not "born" until 1934, when Chairman Ernest Breech installed Kindelberger as its president and general manager. A former chief engineer and vice president of the Douglas Aircraft Company, Kindelberger hired as North American Aviation's chief engineer a man named John Leland "Lee" Atwood. Through the years ahead, Atwood's contributions to North American Aviation would be surpassed by no one, with the sole possible exception of Dutch Kindelberger himself.

Kindelberger and Atwood started from scratch. North American Aviation was a holding company that had never built an airplane of its own. There was little ongoing business other than some bits and pieces left over from its various holdings. There was a little modification work on the Berliner-Joyce P-16 (later PB-1), a biplane for the Army Air Corps, but the plane was already obsolete and out of production.

One useful asset that North American Aviation *had* inherited from the amalgam of companies that had been funneled into it was the staff of excellent craftsmen that Tony Fokker had brought over from Europe. This group formed the nucleus of Kindelberger's plan to launch the former holding company into the real world. Given the option of building aircraft for the commercial market, Kindelberger reasoned that the government market held greater stability in the depths of the Great Depression.

In 1935, the same year that Reuben Fleet moved Consolidated from Buffalo to California, Kindelberger moved North American across the continent from Dundalk, Maryland, to Inglewood, California, a few miles from Santa Monica, where he had worked for Donald Douglas just a year earlier.

Another East Coast planemaker who built his company into an icon of the American aircraft industry was Leroy Randle Grumman. After earning his engineering degree from Cornell University in 1916, Grumman enlisted as an ensign in the U.S. Naval Reserve, became a pilot, and studied aeronautical engineering at MIT at the Navy's expense. In 1920, Grumman became general manager at Loening Aircraft and stayed until 1929. With the help of fellow Loening alums Bill Schwendler and Leon "Jake" Swirbul, Grumman started a new company on Long Island called Grumman Aeronautical Engineering. The company was located at several places on the island before settling on a permanent home at Bethpage in 1937. For the U.S. Navy, the Grumman Company designed the first practical floats with retractable landing gear, and thereafter Navy contracts flowed in large numbers. During

Seen here in December 1926, the wood mill at the Consolidated Aircraft Corporation in Buffalo, New York, was very low-tech by later industry standards. In contrast to what appears to be a technologically primitive environment, the men who worked here were extraordinarily skilled craftsmen. *Author collection*

World War II, Grumman built more combat aircraft for the Navy than anyone. The aircraft were so solid and sturdy, that the company was referred to as the "Grumman Iron Works."

It would be natural to chart parallels between the American automobile industry and the American aviation industry during the early decades of the twentieth century. Both started around the turn of the century, both produced machines that were powered by internal combustion engines, and both were developed by innovative entrepreneurs. There were a few such parallels, but also many differences. While both industries began as craft shops, the American automobile industry had embraced mass production by the 1920s, while planemakers didn't have the orders to truly justify assembly lines.

In the decade leading up to World War II there was little enthusiasm on the part of many planemakers to expand to mass production when their annual unit output was modest. All were aware that in 1929, on the eve of the stock market crash, Glenn Martin had moved into a large new factory at Middle River, near Baltimore, and that he wound up under Section 77B of the Federal Bankruptcy Act on debt that came due in 1934.

During the 1920s and 1930s, the factories of the American aircraft industry were organized very much along the "craft method" lines of production that the American automobile industry had abandoned before World War I. In fact, the planemakers even built their own machine tools. The typical factory floor in the American aircraft industry looked nothing like a Detroit assembly line plant. Though leading-edge equipment such as pneumatic riveters and electric spot-welders were present on the floor, each aircraft was built from the ground up.

Changes to an aircraft design might occur with every dozen aircraft, something that was unheard of in the automobile industry. Aircraft were, in the terminology of the times, "shop engineered." The automakers could not afford such changes on an assembly line, but then they had to produce thousands—or tens of thousands—of units, while an order for 100 aircraft was considered large.

According to Irving Brinton Holley in the Center of Military History study *Buying Aircraft*:

> There were very few entirely vertical corporations in the aircraft industry producing airframes, engines, and all major components, but most airplane manufacturers did not rely heavily upon subcontractors for components and subassemblies. Factors such as the absence of manufacturers willing to accept subcontracts, the limited number of units in production runs, the need for close tolerances in precision work, and the necessity for a high order of production coordination in an area of frequent and rapid design change, as well as the desire of the airframe manufacturers to find employment for idle sections of their own production forces, all contributed to the peacetime practice of minimizing subcontract work. Even such a relatively

large-scale manufacturer as Boeing fabricated all dies for presses, hammers, and drawbenches in Boeing shops.

Because airframes tended to outlast engines by a considerable factor, aircraft enginemakers introduced mass production a decade ahead of the planemakers. In 1930, Pratt & Whitney built a huge factory at East Hartford, Connecticut, with a 1,000-foot assembly line. Holley described the plant, paraphrasing J. W. Marshall's article, "Line Production the Keynote of New Pratt and Whitney Aircraft Plant," that appeared in the July 17, 1930, issue of *Iron Age*:

> The major unit of the Pratt & Whitney plant consisted of a single floor area 1,000 feet long and 400 feet wide. Down the center of this area ran an aisle 15 feet wide. Railroad sidings and truck platforms brought in raw materials at one end of this structure where electric trucks hauled color-coded tote boxes from department to department as fabrication progressed with aluminum machining on one side of the main center aisle and steel machining on the other. Cross aisles facilitated the flow of parts that moved from machining departments to the assembly line where engines grew with the accretion of parts as they moved toward the final inspection point. Beyond the inspection point were located another set of railroad sidings and truck platforms to haul away the finished product.

Moritz Kahn—a vice president with Albert Kahn, Inc., the industrial architectural and engineering firm that played a significant part in subsequent wartime expansion of the aircraft industry—later observed that East Hartford had "followed the lead of Detroit" by pointing the way for the aircraft industry to pursue. Though few of the other 1930 engine factories were as dramatic as Pratt & Whitney's plant, the engine builders were more cognizant than the airframe makers of the need for the efficiencies of an assembly line operation.

In terms of volume, there was no comparison between the American aircraft industry and the automakers. In 1929, on the eve of the Great Depression, the automobile industry produced 5.29 million units, compared to just 6,522 for the aircraft industry. In 1933, at the trough of the Depression, 1.8 million cars were built, compared to just 1,179 airplanes. In 1936, the total value of the products of the American aircraft industry was reckoned at $86 million (approximately $1.2 billion in current dollars), compared to $2.5 billion (approximately $35 billion in current dollars) for the automobile industry, $420 million for farm equipment, and $153 million for typewriters and office equipment.

There were, of course, economies of scale in the automobile industry. A planemaker might pay 20 cents for a radiator cap in lots of 20 because that was all that were needed for a month's production. Meanwhile, automakers were buying in lots of 500 and paying just a dime each.

While the auto industry was abandoning the craft method for building cars, many early aircraft were entirely handmade. These men are building a section of the Boeing Model 6, a one-of-a-kind flying boat that was used for the first international airmail flights between Seattle and Victoria, British Columbia. *Boeing Archives*

Another difference was that there was no aeronautical Detroit, a city that was, and still is, synonymous with the American automobile industry. The aircraft companies had cropped up all over the United States and by the 1930s the industry was highly decentralized. Bell and Curtiss-Wright's Airplane divisions were in Buffalo, while Republic and Grumman were on Long Island. Boeing was based in the distant Northwest. A number of other mainly smaller firms were scattered through the industrial Northeast. Among the larger ones, Brewster was in Johnsville, Pennsylvania; Piper was in Lock Haven, Pennsylvania; Fairchild was in Hagerstown, Maryland; and Glenn Martin was near Baltimore. Beech, Cessna, and Stearman (the latter Boeing-owned after 1929) were all near Wichita, Kansas, but other companies were far distant from the rest of the industry. Smaller manufacturers and parts suppliers were located in about half the states.

Though there was no aeronautical Detroit, a close runner-up would have been Southern California, known within the Golden State itself simply as the "Southland." Consolidated and Ryan were in San Diego, and the sprawling Los Angeles metro area was home to Douglas, Lockheed, Northrop, North American, and Vultee, to name only the major companies.

Chapter Two

Backing into World War II

As Europe began slipping toward World War II in the late 1930s, that continent and the United States were both attempting to climb out of the Great Depression, which had so adversely affected all aspects of economic and commercial life after October 1929.

As with much of American industry, the Depression years were lean ones for the planemakers. There was little commercial work and the government was a frugal customer. From 1931 through 1937, the largest American planemakers did more than half of their business with the military. All of Glenn Martin's business was with the government, and 91 percent of the aircraft built by Douglas were on military contracts. Chance Vought, Consolidated, Curtiss, and Grumman sold between 75 and 79 percent of their aircraft to the military. For Boeing, 59 percent of its aircraft was under military contract.

The Army bought more aircraft than the Navy, but the numbers were small. The acquisition of aircraft by the U.S. Army was governed by the Air Corps Act of July 1926, which created the Air Corps and authorized its strength "not to exceed" 1,800 aircraft, with acquisitions to replace obsolete equipment "not to exceed" 400 annually. Because of maintenance downtime, there were almost never 1,800 aircraft on hand at any time. The U.S. Navy's air arm, meanwhile, was authorized to have a 1,000-plane inventory but had a lot fewer in service most of the time.

During the 1930s, military aircraft in Germany and the United Kingdom tended to be superior both in quantity and quality to those in the United States. The former was true because of the growing arms race between those countries; the latter was true because innovation tended to be stifled by economics. The United States government was unwilling to underwrite the costs of research and development, and planemakers shied away from large investments in leading-edge technology when there was no certainty of production contracts. This was especially true as the costs of developing more and more complex aircraft increased dramatically. However, by the end of the decade, the Air Corps adopted a policy of paying for second- and third-place aircraft that were entered in official design competitions. The first-place aircraft, of course, were awarded production contracts.

The Air Corps constantly lobbied Congress and the executive branch for increases in quantity and quality, and a board of inquiry headed by former Secretary of War Newton Baker concurred in its July 1934 report. Congress, in turn, authorized 2,230 aircraft as a "minimum safe peacetime strength." A bill setting this figure as a maximum rather than a minimum was finally signed into law in 1936 and remained in force until 1939.

Foremost among those who advocated an increase in the strength of the Air Corps was the officer who became its commander in 1938. General Henry Harley "Hap" Arnold had graduated from the U.S. Military Academy at West Point in 1907 and in 1911 was assigned to Wright Field, Ohio, for pilot training with the Army Signal Corps

This was the scene at Boeing's Plant 2 at Boeing Field in Seattle as World War II raged in Europe, and America remained at peace. In the foreground, the wings are being attached to an early model B-17 Flying Fortress, while in the background (left) three commercial Model 307 Stratoliners are taking shape. *Boeing Archives*

President Franklin Delano Roosevelt saw the effectiveness of German airpower in the early days of World War II and became fixed on the notion that the United States' armed forces should have more planes. During the 1930s, Congress authorized 2,230 military aircraft as a "minimum safe peacetime strength." On May 16, 1940, as German armies flooded into France, Roosevelt stunned Congress and the media by calling for 50,000 planes. Then he created the bureaucracy to make it happen. *Franklin D. Roosevelt Library*

nautical Division, the forerunner to the Air Corps that he would eventually command. Through the 1920s and 1930s, he had been one of a number of young officers who believed in the idea that air power was an effective means of defending the United States. By the time Arnold took over command of the Air Corps, it was clear that Germany believed in air power as a key weapon for waging war.

The clouds of war had been gathering over Europe throughout the 1930s. Adolf Hitler came to power as Germany's chancellor in 1933 and began the steps that led to the rearmament of Germany in violation of the Treaty of Versailles that had ended World War I. By 1939, Hitler had absorbed all of Austria and Czechoslovakia into his Third Reich. Britain and France complained loudly but took no action. To many observers, it was clear that war was virtually inevitable and the old adage about preparing for war in order to preserve peace came to mind—often.

In the United States, President Franklin Roosevelt was among those who saw preparation for war as a necessary step. If a prepared

military could not provide peace, at least it could defend against aggression. Though the United States would remain neutral, it was time to start gearing up for what would officially be called "National Defense."

As for military aircraft, the rapid expansion of the German Luftwaffe was seen as emblematic of Hitler's military buildup. With this in mind, the authorized strength of the U.S. Army Air Corps of 2,230 aircraft seemed a bit low. In November 1938, Roosevelt mentioned that perhaps that number ought to be raised to an astounding 20,000, a number that was well above what even General Hap Arnold had dared to suggest to a tightfisted Congress. It was widely rumored that Roosevelt would ask Congress for at least 10,000—half of his trial balloon figure—but in January 1939, he asked for merely 3,000, scarcely more than the current authorization. The politically skillful chief executive had gotten people used to a five-digit number, while pleasing fiscal conservatives with a small request. The net result was that Congress itself looked at Germany, saw the Luftwaffe and Hitler's aggression against Czechoslovakia, and cringed. In April 1939, they authorized an increase to 6,000 aircraft for the Air Corps, although they appropriated funds for fewer than 5,500. The Luftwaffe would take delivery of 8,295 aircraft in 1939 and set their sights on more than 10,000 the following year.

The April 1939 Air Corps authorization appropriated $27 million (approximately $380 million in current dollars) immediately and $31 million for the following fiscal year. An additional $89 million (approximately $1.25 billion in current dollars) was added in July. For the American aircraft industry, where worries had long centered on finding enough work to fill their factories, the fears now turned to having enough floor space to fill the orders that began to flood in. This would lead eventually to the government intervening and underwriting the cost of new manufacturing plants for the major airframe manufacturers and their subcontractors.

There were important reasons for the Congress to authorize industrial mobilization before the United States entered World War II. Most members of its hallowed chambers recalled the experience of World War I: many aspects of the mobilization that began in April 1917 were not yet up to speed when the war ended in November 1918. Shortages of parts and subassemblies were only part of the industrial chaos that had resulted.

To assess what could be accomplished in terms of increasing American aircraft industry output, analysts looked at two precedents. The first was in World War I, when production increased from 400 aircraft in 1916 to around 2,000 in 1917 and about 14,000 in 1918. The second example was the boom period from 1926 to the stock market crash of 1929, when the annual output of the American aircraft industry increased from 1,156 to 6,522. The latter was the most realistic comparison, and it turned out to be accurate.

As the United States mobilized its industrial plant, the War Department and the Air Corps, in particular, initially adopted the concept of creating industrial *capacity* rather than building hardware. In other words, the idea was to encourage the expansion of factories that would be *ready* to build airplanes rather than to actually build airplanes. In retrospect, this may not have been a bad idea. As a case in point, the Air Corps officially allocated 37 percent of the production capacity to building observation planes, a type for which there was very little tactical need during World War II. To have built them ahead of time would have been a waste of resources.

As the American aircraft industry geared up to produce aircraft for the United States armed forces, the equivalent industries in Britain and France were well into a rearmament effort that stretched their capacities to the limit. Because both of these nations understood and respected the enormous mass-production capability of American industry, representatives of both countries knocked at the doors of American planemakers. In Burbank, Lockheed adapted its Super Electra as a patrol bomber called the Hudson for the Royal Air Force. Across the hill in Santa Monica, the French jumpstarted the Douglas DB-7 program, which became the A-20 program, the Douglas warplane produced in the largest numbers in the company's history.

During the first quarter of 1939, the two leading western European powers placed orders for more than 1,200 aircraft from Curtiss, Douglas, Martin, North American Aviation, and others. Other countries followed the lead of the big two, as Australia, Belgium, Canada, Norway, and Sweden came shopping. For the American planemakers, these orders helped pay for plant expansion that would later benefit the American armed forces. American workers were also gaining experience and American engineers would soon benefit from the combat careers of American aircraft flying under foreign flags.

On September 1, 1939, having signed a nonaggression pact with the Soviet Union, Hitler launched a full-scale attack on Poland. Britain and France issued ultimatums because their mutual-assistance treaties with Poland finally called for them to take action to halt Hitler's aggression. On September 3, Britain and France declared that a state of war had existed for two days.

At the time Germany invaded Poland, its army and Luftwaffe were the most well trained, best equipped, and overall superior military forces in the world. Their coordinated air and ground offensive, known as *blitzkrieg* ("lightning war"), was the most rapid and efficient military attack the world had ever seen. Fast-moving tanks, mobile forces, dive bombers, and paratroop units all working together as one tight, well-disciplined force stunned the world, especially the Polish defenders. Germany subjugated Poland in just three weeks. The Luftwaffe played such a crucial role in this action that it surprised air power advocates and air power skeptics alike.

After Germany had conquered Poland, Britain and France dispatched a few bombers over Germany, but for the most part, took no offensive action. A lull in the action of World War II descended over Europe.

General Henry Harley "Hap" Arnold headed the U.S. Army Air Corps (USAAF after June 1941) from 1938 through the end of World War II. He oversaw a 40-fold increase in the strength of his force and commanded the largest air force in history. He is pictured here with the five-star rank to which he was promoted in December 1944. *U.S. Air Force*

Throughout the winter of 1939 and 1940, Allied and German troops sat and stared at one another across the heavily fortified Franco-German border. So little happened that newspaper writers dubbed the situation the *sitzkrieg* or the "phony war." As Europe watched the *sitzkrieg* with a mixture of uncertainty and incredulity, the governments of Britain and France set their sights on acquiring the weapons of war. In San Diego, they bought Liberator bombers from Consolidated. On Long Island, they bought Wildcat fighters from Grumman and renamed them Martlets.

These shopping trips were conducted under a cloud of legal ambiguity and a shroud of secrecy. The isolationist contingent in the U.S. Congress was anxious that the United States stay out of and as far away as possible from "Europe's War." It was not until early 1940 that the American aircraft industry was officially allowed to freely market its products to foreign countries involved in World War II. By this time, overseas orders accounted for more business among American planemakers than the United States armed forces.

The Airplane Division of Curtiss-Wright dedicated its new Port Columbus, Ohio, factory three days before the Pearl Harbor attack. It had actually been building airplanes here for nearly six weeks. *Author collection*

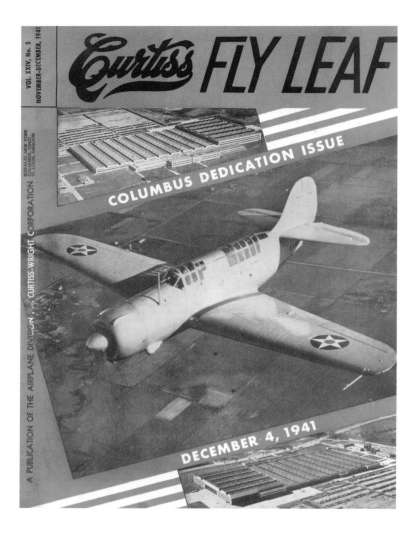

Suddenly, on April 9, 1940, Germany attacked. *Sitzkrieg* became *blitzkrieg* once again. German troops quickly occupied Denmark and Norway. On May 10, the Germans began a great offensive to the west that duplicated their advance on Belgium and France in 1914 at the beginning of World War I. By May 28, Luxembourg, Belgium, and the Netherlands had surrendered and German forces were pouring into France. By June 14, Germany had seized control of Paris, having accomplished in five weeks what it had been unable to do in four years of protracted fighting in World War I.

France finally surrendered on June 22, leaving Britain to face the onslaught of Germany's blitzkrieg alone. Only 21 miles of English Channel separated Germany's crack troops from an army that had abandoned all of its equipment in France when it barely managed to escape the Germans at Dunkirk on the French coast on June 4.

While Hitler's forces prepared for a cross-channel invasion of Britain, the English people rallied around Prime Minister Winston Churchill, who had taken office on May 10, telling them he had "nothing to offer but blood, toil, tears and sweat." He defied Hitler, even as the Luftwaffe began a brutal, unremitting bombing assault on Britain's ports, factories, and cities. The only thing that stood in the way of an easy victory was the courageous but vastly outnumbered pilots of the Royal Air Force, who met the Germans like gnats attacking crows. Despite the fact that the British had fewer than 1,000 fighters to face a Luftwaffe onslaught four times as large, the RAF destroyed 12 bombers for each of their own losses. Churchill called it the RAF's "finest hour."

More than anything else, the Battle of Britain demonstrated the profound and significant role that would henceforth be played by air power in modern warfare.

Even as the Germans swallowed Norway, Denmark, Belgium, and the Netherlands, and swarmed into France, the American people wanted to stay out of the war. However, many were now starting to worry and there was a growing realization that isolation might not be possible. The United States and its aircraft industry were backing slowly into World War II.

On May 16, 1940, two days after the Netherlands government fled in disarray, Hitler's *blitzkrieg* was on the move and France teetered on the brink of collapse. This was the same day that President Roosevelt went before Congress and raised the ante on military aircraft. Sixteen months earlier he had floated the figure of 10,000 aircraft and asked for 3,000. This time he came right out and proposed that Congress authorize funding for 50,000.

In July 1940, with the German armies in control of most of Western Europe and England seeming to be ripe for the picking, the United States government and military services were faced with the problem of expanding the Army and Navy and the air services of both. In July, Army and Navy planners studied the practical side of arriving at Roosevelt's figure of 50,000, deciding on a 73/27 split. Of its 36,500-unit target, the U.S. Army Air Corps still had around 7,700 undelivered aircraft from 1939 and 1940 orders, so 28,000 units became the official target and April 1942 the target date.

American aircraft industry expansion took place against the backdrop of the general mobilization for war by all American industry that had begun in 1939. Under the National Defense Program, plans were laid for an expansion of all essential industries.

To aid the government in this industrial expansion, the Roosevelt administration created the National Defense Advisory Commission in May 1940. The idea was to bring experienced industry leaders on board to organize the effort. To head this commission and serve as commissioner of production, Roosevelt tapped William Signius "Big Bill" Knudsen. An expert on mass production and a skilled manager, he had been an executive at the Ford Motor Company and had served as president of General Motors since 1937. In 1942, Knudsen would be commissioned as a lieutenant general in the U.S. Army. Knudsen hired specialists in a wide range of fields, including industrial materials, industrial production, employment, farm produce, transportation, price stabilization, and consumer protection. Staffs were formed and extensive studies were made of what might be required.

Planemakers, like other industries, were given quotas of military equipment. This meant that new factories had to be built and Congress authorized funds for expansion of existing facilities and for new factories that would be government-owned but operated by individual manufacturers at new locations. All of this would be managed from the government side by a new bureaucracy known as the Defense Plant Corporation.

The government also adopted a policy of industrial decentralization, so new locations were selected for aircraft expansion plants and existing factory complexes were added on to. In 1940, nearly 90 percent of airframe manufacturing capacity measured in square feet of floor space was located in five states with 65 percent along or near one of the coasts. California alone had 44 percent. Because the flagship plants were near the coasts and potentially susceptible to possible enemy attack, most new factories would be located far inland.

The idea of tapping the vast capacity and expertise of the Detroit automakers to address the need for airplanes was naturally on the minds of everyone in the Army and Navy who was involved in military aircraft procurement. Certainly with automobile industrialist Big Bill Knudsen serving as Roosevelt's production tsar, this idea was an obvious one. The United States automobile industry was the global standard for high-volume production of complex machinery. They built more cars than were built in any other country on earth, and in 1937 had produced 1,600 cars for every airplane turned out by the American aircraft industry. They understood mass production, of course, but they also had a well-oiled machine in place for ordering and processing parts, accessories, and subassemblies. They also had immense capacity in terms of labor, engineering talent, floor space, and machine tools.

In October 1940, Knudsen began a round of meetings in New York and Detroit with automobile industry executives to discuss the idea of the automakers becoming planemakers. He also hosted a summit conference of the heads of the major aircraft companies to discuss the automobile industry's possible role in manufacturing aircraft and subassemblies for aircraft.

While the two industries focused on bomber production, an innovative plan came from labor with regard to smaller and less complex fighter aircraft. In December 1940, Walter Reuther, head of the United Auto Workers (UAW) union, proposed a plan whereby his members and the automobile industry could gear up to produce 500 fighters per *day*. Reuther suggested that this would be possible if the industry both agreed to pool all of its machine tools and forgo the traditional annual model-year changes for 1941 and 1942. To supervise this process, he

March 25, 1941. Third of steel up. Roof appears.

July 21, 1941. First third of parking lot surfaced. Factory in final stages.

April 8, 1941. West end of building takes shape. Steel at half way point.

August 5, 1941. Parking lot complete. Factory roof finished.

May 10, 1941. Roof started in factory high-bay area.

September 9, 1941. Property ready for grading and clearance.

June 17, 1941. Office and factory moved in day before picture.

September 27, 1941. Ground cleared. Sidewalks and roadways in.

July 3, 1941. Office-engineering building practically complete.

October 16, 1941. An impressive plant. Production well under way.

This series of photographs shows the progress of the work at the Curtiss Port Columbus facility. Completed in 147 days, the plant had 840,000 square feet of manufacturing space. Ground was broken on November 28, 1940. *Author collection*

suggested a nine-member board that would have equal representation from the government, the industry, and the UAW.

Against a backdrop of animosity between the industry and the UAW that dated back to the 1930s, Reuther's plan was eventually rejected. The Air Corps voted against the plan because of its desire for increased capacity for bombers rather than fighters. Within a year, the practice of foregoing the model-year change would come to pass, however. After a mere handful of 1942 models, there would not be a new model year again until a few automakers brought out an abbreviated number of 1945 model cars.

By 1940, it seemed to Knudsen and others that the automobile industry, based on its immense size, ought to be able to handle at least as much airplane production, if not *more*, than the American aircraft industry. But it never happened. Ultimately, the large-scale involvement of the American automobile industry in building aircraft was limited to a few factories, including the New Jersey facilities of the Eastern Aircraft

LEFT: Boeing used this billboard on East Marginal Way South in Seattle to celebrate the firm's prowess in the field of four-engine aircraft. Pictured are the Model 314 Clipper and Model 307 Stratoliner, led by a Model 299 (B-17) Flying Fortress. *Boeing Archives*

OPPOSITE: Maryland II bombers destined for Britain's Royal Air Force are seen on the factory floor at the Glenn Martin facility in Middle River, Maryland, in December 1940. *Glenn L. Martin Company*

Division of General Motors, and Ford's all-new bomber plant at Willow Run near Detroit.

At the end of 1941, the major automakers formed the Automotive Council for War Production to coordinate their contribution to the war effort, but those contributions would be mainly outside the aviation sector. The reasons that the automakers were not more deeply involved were many and practical. For example, only a tiny fraction of the large tools and dies used in the two industries were compatible. The automobile industry was accustomed to working with steel, which has much different properties than aluminum, which is easier to form. The planemakers were also used to working with more precise tolerances. And, of course, most existing automobile assembly lines were too narrow for the large aircraft the Air Corps wanted most.

Another factor that made the automakers less than enthusiastic was the issue of unscheduled and unschedulable changes. Theoretically, the automobile industry could achieve huge production totals; but to make changes and upgrades, assembly lines had to be stopped. The American aircraft industry was used to these stoppages, but the automobile industry typically froze a design and made it exactly the same way for one year until the annual new model was introduced. Without freezing a design—a virtual impossibility with aircraft—a Detroit-style rapid production rate could not be achieved.

The American automobile industry was much more suited to military vehicles, which were soon coming off the Detroit assembly lines by the tens of thousands. The members of the Automotive Council for War Production did, however, build very large numbers of aircraft engines. Among them, Buick, Chevrolet, and Ford eventually produced nearly 200,000 radial engines under license from Pratt & Whitney (more than Pratt & Whitney itself), while Packard built 54,714 Merlin inline engines under license from Rolls-Royce in England. A great deal of plant expansion took place with regard to aircraft engines. Among these was a 6.75-million-square-foot plant constructed by the Dodge Division of Chrysler Corporation in Chicago to build 18,349 Wright Cyclone radial aircraft engines.

The Curtiss-Wright Corporation, the successor to America's first two major planemakers, still ranked among the industry leaders. Its Wright Engine Division produced the great Wright Cyclone, one of the most widely used American radial engines of the 1930s and 1940s.

RIGHT: Boeing President Philip G. "Phil" Johnson and company founder Bill Boeing enjoy a smoke during the happier times that preceded the company's divestiture of its airline holdings. *Boeing Archives*

FAR RIGHT: Clairmont L. "Claire" Egtvedt served as both president and acting chairman of Boeing through much of the 1930s and 1940s and remained in the top job until 1966. During the war years, he made his home in the 3100 block of Lakewood Avenue in Seattle, an easy drive from his office. *Boeing Archives*

Meanwhile, its Airplane Division had been a key supplier to the U.S. Army Air Corps and the U.S. Navy during the 1930s. Curtiss produced myriad single-engine biplane combat aircraft for both services. Indeed, 15 of the pursuit aircraft that the Air Corps acquired in its P-1 through P-23 series were Curtiss products, mainly Curtiss Hawks. In 1935, Curtiss first flew its Model 75 monoplane fighter, which was widely marketed both to the U.S. Army Air Corps (as P-36) and to customers around the world. Eventually the Hawk would be the first American airplane of which more than 1,000 were produced.

As World War II began in Europe, the Aircraft Division was producing the Curtiss P-40 Warhawk, the standard frontline fighter in the U.S. Army. In fact, through 1942, more P-40s were produced in the United States than all other fighter types combined. The aircraft was also acquired by Britain's Royal Air Force under the names Tomahawk and Kittyhawk.

On December 4, 1941, the Thursday before the Sunday of Pearl Harbor, Curtiss auspiciously opened a sprawling new factory complex at Columbus, Ohio. In July 1940, the National Defense Program had handed Curtiss-Wright substantial new orders, but because of the industrial decentralization policy, Curtiss had to build a new factory rather than expand the one at Buffalo to handle the new orders. Charles Loos, vice president of the Curtiss-Wright Corporation in New York

Crews at the Douglas Aircraft facility in Santa Monica, California, assemble one of the DC-3 airliners that the company delivered to Pan American in 1937.
Courtesy Harry Gann

City, together with Peter Jansen, general factory manager of the Airplane Division, led a tour of several Midwest cities, finally selecting a large tract of land near the Port Columbus airport. Lester Waugh of the Reconstruction Finance Corporation approved the site, and the Columbus city council held a special meeting in November 1940 to grant a lease to Curtiss-Wright and the Defense Plant Corporation.

The Curtiss Port Columbus complex was a typical case study of the many factories constructed under the auspices of the Defense Plant Corporation. A contemporary Curtiss-Wright chronicle of the project described the facility as:

an outstanding model of efficient, peacetime industrial design. In the factory over 300,000 square feet of heat resistant cobalt glass carries daylight to the workers—light without eye-straining glare. During the day a complex system of fluorescent illumination spreads light evenly into every nook and corner of the plant and at night transforms the midnight darkness into noonday sunlight. Huge ducts converging in a master control room located in the basement provide forced draft ventilation so that regardless of blistering summer sun or blustering winter winds, the 840,000 square feet of actual manufacturing space is automatically heated and ventilated.

RIGHT: John Knudsen "Jack" Northrop, seen here in a 1935 portrait, started his brilliant aeronautical engineering career with the Loughead brothers in 1916 at the age of 21. He became Don Douglas' chief engineer in 1923. Northrop was involved in numerous ventures before starting his third and final company in 1939. *Author collection*

OPPOSITE: A commercial Model 10 Electra nears completion at the Lockheed factory in Burbank, California, in 1934. Amelia Earhart flew a modified Model 10 on her most famous flights. *Lockheed California Company*

It was at Columbus that Curtiss began production of the most widely used American dive bomber of the war. Ordered by the U.S. Navy under the scout bomber designation, the SB2C was named the Helldiver, an appellation recycled from several earlier Navy aircraft.

The Glenn L. Martin Company had closed its Cleveland, Ohio, factory in 1929 to concentrate operations at the new factory in Middle River, Maryland, southeast of Baltimore. During this period and into the 1930s, Martin produced a line of biplane torpedo bombers for the U.S. Navy. By 1932, Martin was also developing its B-10 and B-12 twin-engine monoplane bombers. Innovative for their time, these bombers were long obsolete by World War II. As the war approached, however, Martin received sizable export orders from Britain's RAF for its Maryland and Baltimore twin-engine light bombers. By World War II, Martin was developing a series of large flying boats for the U.S. Navy.

Out West, Boeing had grown considerably during the 1920s and 1930s, although the company would make a major change in direction in 1934. On the military side, Boeing was Curtiss' only major competitor in the business of building pursuit planes. Its similar P-12 and F4B were the standard biplane fighters for the Army and Navy until the 1930s. On the commercial side, Boeing developed several important

aircraft, but Bill Boeing's dream had been for an integrated manufacturing and airline company. He created Boeing Air Transport 1927 with an east-west route between San Francisco and Chicago. A year later, Boeing acquired Pacific Air Transport (PAT), which had a north-south route between Seattle and Los Angeles via San Francisco. In October 1928, the Boeing Airplane & Transport Corporation (BATC) was incorporated as a holding company for BAT and PAT, as well as the Boeing Company. Early in 1929, BATC became the United Aircraft & Transport Corporation (UATC) and acquired several new subsidiaries, including Igor Sikorsky's successful seaplane company, aircraft engine-maker Pratt & Whitney, the Hamilton Standard Propeller Company, and the Chance Vought Corporation.

In 1930, UATC bought National Air Transport (NAT), an airline serving points from New York to Texas, and Varney Airlines, a major regional carrier in the West. In March 1931, United Air Lines was created as a management corporation to coordinate the operations of all of UATC's airline subsidiaries.

Bill Boeing's United Air Lines became an operating company in May 1934, but within weeks, the Airmail Act of 1934 formally prohibited the same company from owning both airlines and aircraft manufacturing companies. UATC was dissolved. The airlines were spun off under the umbrella of the United Air Lines Transport Corporation (UALTC), operating as United Air Lines. Pratt & Whitney, Hamilton Standard, Sikorsky, and Chance Vought, all based in Connecticut, were separated from the airline and rolled into an entity known as United Aircraft. Boeing went back to its premerger form as strictly a Seattle-based aircraft-manufacturing company. Displeased with this turn of events, founder William Edward Boeing left the company permanently.

By 1940, the Boeing Company could—and did—boast that it had become a world leader, if not *the* world leader, in the design and manufacture of large four-engine aircraft. Its pressurized Model 307 Stratoliner and its huge Model 314 Clipper flying boat were milestones of commercial air travel, and its XB-15 and B-17 bombers were among the largest military aircraft in the world.

When Bill Boeing left the company in 1934, the men who led Boeing into its new era of industry leadership were Clairmont L. "Claire" Egtvedt and Philip G. "Phil" Johnson, a pair of engineers turned businessmen whom Boeing had hired in 1917 as they graduated from the University of Washington School of Engineering. Johnson became the plant superintendent in 1920 and was named vice president in 1921. In 1926, he became president of the Boeing Company and played a key role in developing the firm's network of airline holdings. In 1933, he left Seattle to serve as president of Boeing subsidiary United Air Lines, and later as head of the Boeing-owned holding company, the United Aircraft & Transport Company. When Boeing was compelled to divest itself of airline operations in 1934, Phil Johnson moved north to help organize Trans Canada Airways.

Lockheed Hudson bombers for Britain's Royal Air Force take shape on the Burbank assembly line in 1940. When World War II began, the armed forces of both Britain and France made shopping trips to the United States to acquire aircraft. *Lockheed California Company*

Egtvedt, meanwhile, worked his way up to the role of chief engineer and in 1926 became vice president and general manager. In 1933, he succeeded Phil Johnson as president of Boeing and when Bill Boeing resigned as chairman a year later, Egtvedt took on the added responsibility of acting chairman of the board. During the 1930s, he led the company through the quagmire of the Great Depression and into the field of four-engine aircraft.

Johnson returned as president of Boeing in 1939 on the eve of World War II and Egtvedt was officially named chairman. As described in the August 2, 1943, issue of *Time* magazine, "Burly, tireless Philip Gustav Johnson became president of Boeing Airplane for the second time in his life. His first term ended in 1934, when Boeing was part of United Aircraft, and Johnson, as United president, became a scapegoat in the federal government's abortive 1934 airmail contract cancellation. When Boeing recalled him from Canadian exile five years later, the company was suffering from two interrelated problems: 1) sales were small, its profit & loss statement soaked in red ink; 2) production was painstakingly perfectionist and inefficient."

Under Johnson's leadership and management abilities, Boeing created a production machine of unprecedented scale.

Boeing's signature warplane through most of World War II was the extraordinary B-17 Flying Fortress. It first flew in 1935, with its design having benefited greatly from the engineering work that Boeing had done on the XB-15, the even larger bomber that was part of an early U.S. Army Air Corps research program aimed at the development of very-long-range bombers. The XB-15 was large and impractical, but

Hulls for PBY Catalina flying boats take shape at the Consolidated Aircraft facility on the shores of San Diego Bay, July 20, 1936. *Author collection*

the four-engine B-17 became one of history's greatest aircraft. Designed by a team led by Ed Wells, the B-17 (Boeing Model 299) addressed a U.S. Army Air Corps request for a bomber with a 1-ton bomb load, an air speed in excess of 200 miles per hour, and a range in excess of 2,000 miles. Specifically, the Air Corps wanted a "multi-engine" aircraft. In January 1936, the Air Corps ordered 13 service-test aircraft under the designation Y1B-17, and later added 39 B-17Bs. Meanwhile, the Air Corps had ordered 133 twin-engine Douglas Model DB-1s under the designation B-18. Because of the Byzantine government contracting practices of the 1930s, the Air Corps budget could accept more B-18s because the unit cost was lower.

When World War II began in Europe in 1939, the U.S. Army began planning for the long-range defense of the Western Hemisphere against

possible Axis incursion. By now, evaluation of the Flying Fortress had indicated that it would be the key heavy bomber. In 1940, the Air Corps ordered 80 Model 299H aircraft designated B-17C and B-17D.

In California during the 1930s, Douglas completely revolutionized commercial air travel with the DC-1 through DC-3 series of large twin-engine monoplane propliners. The DC-1 first flew in 1933, and the DC-2 (essentially the production version of the DC-1) in 1934. The Douglas Skysleeper Transport (DST), which first flew on December 17, 1935, was redesignated as the DC-3 when configured as a day-use, nonsleeper offering luxury and reliability that could not have been imagined only a few years before. Even before World War II began, the U.S. Army Air Corps (U.S. Army Air Forces after June 1941) and the U.S. Navy started to acquire DC-2s and DC-3s to satisfy their needs for transport aircraft.

Bulkhead sections for the inside of PBY Catalinas are finished by crews at Consolidated in San Diego. They'll soon be placed in the hull that will be built up in the nearest production bay. *Author collection*

During World War II, they were purchased primarily under the U.S. Army Air Forces designation C-47 and the Navy designation R4D.

On the military side, Douglas programs in the mid- to late 1930s included the Model DB-1 bomber, which had an airframe adapted from the DC-3 and was acquired by the U.S. Army Air Corps under the designation B-18. For the U.S. Navy, Douglas developed the TBD-1 torpedo bomber, one of the first monoplanes designed for aircraft carrier operations.

Aside from the DC-3, one of the best moves that Don Douglas made in the 1930s was to invest (51 percent of the capital) in the company started by Jack Northrop, the brilliant designer who had worked for both Douglas and Lockheed off and on. The Northrop factory was conveniently located in the coastal town of El Segundo, California, a half hour south of Santa Monica and adjacent to Mines Field (today's Los Angeles International Airport). Northrop was producing the Delta and Gamma commercial aircraft, as well as a series of military aircraft,

ABOVE: Looking every inch the central casting image of a captain of industry, Reuben Hollis Fleet was exactly that. He joined Gallaudet Aircraft as general manager in 1922 and took it over a year later. Consolidating it with other companies, he formed Consolidated Aircraft in 1923. In 1941, he sold his interest for more than $10 million. In the meantime, he became a private consultant to President Roosevelt, who had a special direct-line telephone installed for Fleet. In 1961, he founded the San Diego Aerospace Museum. Fleet died in 1975 at the age of 88. *Author collection*

LEFT: In the final assembly step for PBY Catalinas at Consolidated, seen here in November 1936, wings, engines, and tails were mated with hulls. *Author collection*

including sturdy, low-winged, single-engine attack bombers. Among these were the U.S. Army Air Corps A-13 (Northrop Model 2C) and A17 (Northrop Model 8) series.

Meanwhile, at Inglewood, also next to Mines Field and a short distance east of Jack Northrop's operation, another former Douglas employee was starting to build airplanes. Dutch Kindelberger's North American Aviation had moved west from Maryland in 1935 with little in the way of a track record, but the company had managed to secure a

contract for a new U.S. Army Air Corps basic trainer. The North American Model NA-16 made its first flight in 1935 and earned an Army order for 42 units under the designation BT-9 and with the given name Yale. The production variant would be produced at Inglewood as Model NA-19. The Yale put North American Aviation on the map as a planemaker and went on to evolve into several other groups of similar trainer aircraft. The last major member of the Yale family was the BT14 series, which debuted in 1939.

Low-tech construction methods at a leading-edge factory complex. The plant expansion program undertaken by Consolidated in San Diego in 1939 and 1940 relied on 2-horsepower equipment. The facility would see the construction of thousands of B-24 bombers during World War II, and numerous commercial and military aircraft in the 1950s. Much of the plant was demolished in the 1990s. *Author collection*

A short distance north of Inglewood, El Segundo, and Santa Monica, Lockheed was expanding its operations around the Burbank Airport. The Lockheed Aircraft Company formed by Allan Loughhead in 1926 had gone through a series of owners and financial hard times and was finally acquired in 1932 by a group of investors headed by Robert and Courtland Gross and was reconstituted as the Lockheed Corporation. The company was focusing its attention on a family of sturdy, twin-engine transport aircraft, including the Model 10 Electra, the Model 12 Electra Junior, the Model 14 Super Electra, and the Model 18 Lodestar. Amelia Earhart had flown her Electra on many record-breaking flights before she (and it) disappeared in 1937. Howard Hughes flew his Model 14 in his own record-breaking, three-day, round-the-world flight in 1938. Though Lockheed had relatively little military work for the American armed forces in the 1930s, the British RAF came to Burbank in 1938 to acquire the Hudson, a military derivative of the Lodestar. It would be widely used as a patrol bomber during the coming global conflict.

If betting on Jack Northrop was one of the best moves made by Don Douglas, then the best personnel choice made by Bob Gross during the 1930s was Clarence Leonard "Kelly" Johnson, who would go on to be recognized as one of the foremost aircraft designers of the twentieth century. Johnson grew up around Ishpeming, Michigan, and graduated from the University of Michigan in 1932 with a degree in aeronautical engineering. The following year, at the age of 23, he began his career with Lockheed, working under chief engineer Hall Hibbard. Johnson helped to design the Lockheed Orion single-engine transport and the Model 10 Electra. He quickly developed a reputation as an ingenious engineer and in 1937 the Institute of Aeronautical Sciences (now the American Institute of Aeronautics and Astronautics) awarded him the Sperry Award for his design of the Lockheed-Fowler Flap used in the control surfaces of aircraft. Later in the 1930s, Johnson directed the engineering effort that led to the design of the revolutionary Lockheed P-38 Lightning, the fastest American fighter in the first half of World War II.

Reuben Fleet had brought Consolidated Aircraft west to San Diego for good weather, proximity to a major Navy base, and a never-frozen body of water on which to test and deliver the flying boats that had become a Consolidated specialty. The site chosen was next to Lindbergh Field, so named because it was where Charles Lindbergh had taken delivery of the Ryan NYP known as the *Spirit of St. Louis*. To facilitate the planned flying boat operations, Consolidated's Building 1, a 247,000-square-foot, continuous-flow factory, was just a stone's throw from the tide flats adjacent to San Diego Bay.

When Consolidated opened for business in September 1935, it employed 874 people, including many who had come from Buffalo and 463 who were the first of more than 100,000 San Diegans who would make Consolidated the city's largest civilian employer for the next half century. The first new Consolidated aircraft produced in San Diego was the Catalina, the brainchild of Isaac "Mac" Laddon. The prototype for the new flying boat first flew in 1935. Originally given the patrol desig-

nation XP3Y-1 by the U.S. Navy, the Catalina entered service as the PBY (Patrol Bomber, Consolidated).

The first production PBY was launched on San Diego Bay in October 1936, and with a Navy order for 60 additional Catalinas, Consolidated enlarged the factory, boosting the production area to 543,000 square feet, including an enclosed paved yard where overflow final assembly operations could be conducted in the California sunshine.

As Fleet's Consolidated Aircraft was spreading its wings in San Diego, up the coast in the Los Angeles suburb of Downey, a future "partner" of Consolidated was spreading his wings. Airplane designer Gerard Frebairn "Jerry" Vultee had secured the financial support of Errett Lobban Cord, the self-styled "boy wonder of Wall Street," who owned or controlled the Cord, Duesenberg, and Auburn automobile companies, as well as Stinson Aircraft, Century Airlines, Lycoming Motors, and American Airlines. In 1934 Vultee created the Aviation Company (Avco) as an umbrella for his holdings. Vultee was named vice president and chief engineer of Avco.

Aviation Pioneer Jerry Vultee

Gerard Frebairn "Jerry" Vultee was one of the great entrepreneurs who made early American aviation so interesting. Born in Brooklyn, New York, in 1900, he grew up in Ocean Park, California. He surfed with Duke Kahanamoku and he studied engineering at the California Institute of Technology with Nobel laureate Dr. Robert Millikan. Vultee met Jack Northrop while working at Douglas and moved to Lockheed with him in 1927 to work on the great Lockheed Vega and Air Express.

In June 1928, when Jack Northrop resigned as Lockheed's chief engineer to pursue his own projects, Jerry Vultee took his place. It was in this role that he worked with Charles Lindbergh to design the Sirius low-wing monoplane. He also created the airplane that Wiley Post used to set and then break the round-the-world speed record. By 1934, backed by Errett Lobban Cord, Vultee headed his own factory in Downey, California. Newly wed in January 1935 to Sylvia Parker, daughter of filmographer and production designer Max Parker, Vultee set a speed record in his V-1A on their honeymoon trip to Mexico City.

At age 37, Vultee was on the threshold of an even more fruitful career when he and Sylvia flew to Washington, D.C., in Jerry's Stinson Reliant to pitch the Army on a military derivative of his V-11. In January 1938, on the way back to California, they took off into a snowstorm from Winslow, Arizona. Less than an hour later, the Reliant crashed into Mount Wilson near Flagstaff. Jerry and Sylvia were dead, and their infant son, Peter, was an orphan.

Jerry Vultee was instrumental in the design of several record-setting prewar airplanes, in the process laying the groundwork for many of the great U.S.-built aircraft of World War II. He and his wife Sylvia were killed in a plane crash in January 1938. *Author collection*

Within three years, he was heading his own factory, the Vultee Aircraft Division, in Downey, California, with more than $1 million in orders for V-1s, V-1As, and V-11s. Vultee died tragically in 1938, but the Army ordered the V-11 under the designation YA-19, and Avco spun Jerry's company off as the separate Vultee Aircraft Corporation in 1939. A year later, it purchased the Stinson Aircraft Company that had been started by Eddie Stinson in 1926 and which was responsible for the legendary Detroiter series of early airliners. Like Jerry Vultee, Eddie Stinson died young and well before his full potential could be realized.

Building on the same basic low-wing monoplane design of the V-11, Dick Palmer had created the Vultee Valiant training aircraft that

were sold to the U.S. Army as the BT-13 and BT-15, and to the Navy as the SNV.

The catalyst that led to the merger of Vultee with the much larger Consolidated was Reuben Fleet's response to government procrastination in paying promised reimbursements for aircraft plant expansion. Fleet's fuming disgust finally boiled over in the fall of 1940 when he was at the summit conference of leading planemakers called by Big Bill Knudsen to discuss the automobile industry's role in aviation if the United States entered the war. At this meeting, Fleet brought up the issue of being reimbursed for the first round of the Consolidated's plant expansions. The company had completed construction and submitted its invoice, but no repayment on the $2.47 million (approximately $34 million in current dollars) had come through from the Treasury Department. Fleet had asked Undersecretary of the Navy James Forrestal to pay the bill, audit it later, and deduct irregularities from future invoices.

"They expected me to holler, and I did." Fleet recalled later. "Knudsen called on us around the table for comment. When he got to me, I said it was obvious we would have to use the automobile industry to get anywhere near all the planes we would need. But I said I thought a bigger question was whether you could bank on Uncle Sam's word anymore. I told them about waiting eight and one-half months. I said if I weren't compelled to use dollar bills bearing [Treasury Secretary] Henry Morgenthau's signature, I'd certainly look upon them as being worthless. Forrestal spoke up and said, 'Don't blame Secretary Morgenthau, your invoices are all on my desk. The Navy Department hasn't worked out a procedure to pay you.'"

Fleet got his check at the end of the same day, but he was growing increasingly annoyed by what he saw as "meddling" from government defense mobilization agencies and the "near-confiscatory" tax burden that he carried as chairman, president, and general stockholder.

Finally, in the summer of 1941, Fleet made the decision to step down from the helm of the company that he had created and retire at the relatively young age of 54. He noted that he "couldn't see carrying that load of poles any longer."

In August 1941, Fleet began the negotiations with Victor Emanuel, the president of the Avco holding company, which would lead to a sale of his 34.26 percent share in Consolidated. Avco and Reuben Fleet agreed in November 1941—two weeks before Pearl Harbor—that Vultee would buy Fleet's interest in Consolidated for $10.9 million (approximately $145 million in current dollars).

On the whole, 1941 would be a very good one for the American aircraft industry in terms of earnings, although investment in plant and equipment had kept profits low during the first half of the year. The August 25, 1941, issue of *Time* reported that "Despite the industry's terrific production pace, its first-half profits rose less than run-of-the-mill industrials. Five top-flight plane builders (Curtiss-Wright, Douglas, Martin, North American, United) netted $27,229,000 in the first six

Several PBY Catalinas and a PB2Y Coronado (right) in the final assembly yard at Consolidated on a sunny January day in 1939. The weather was the secret weapon of California planemakers. *Author collection*

months, only 21 percent over 1940. But a cross-section of United States industry (135 motors, steels, oils, etc.) was able to boost profits 30 percent. Taxes were most obviously to blame—chiefly the excess-profits tax, which feeds on the aircraft industry."

However, those taxes would make their way back into the coffers of the planemakers. In 1940, the expenditure from appropriations of the U.S. Army Air Corps had been $605 million (approximately $8.4 billion in current dollars), up from $108 million in 1939 (approximately $1.5 billion in current dollars). In 1941, they were $2.6 billion (approximately $34.7 billion in current dollars).

As the United States industry and armed forces mobilized for the war that seemed inevitable, the U.S. Army took the necessary step of granting its air arm the autonomy that it would need to be effective in the coming conflict. Air power advocates had long favored an air force independent of the U.S. Army, as was the case in Britain with the RAF and in Germany with the Luftwaffe. This would not become a reality until 1947, two years after the war ended, but on June 20, 1941, the air power advocates got the next best thing. President Roosevelt signed the War Powers Act that, among other things, transformed the dependent U.S. Army Air Corps into the autonomous, if not yet independent, U.S. Army Air Forces.

Foremost among those who had advocated air arm independence was Air Corps commander General Hap Arnold, who had also long stumped for the enlargement of the air arm from a token force to one that had true war-winning potential.

In 1941, with the creation of the U.S. Army Air Forces, Arnold became its commander, and when the Joint Chiefs of Staff was formed, Arnold represented the USAAF with a seat at the same table as the commanders of the Army and Navy.

In the summer of 1941 as the new air arm relished its autonomy, it also relished the fact that it was on its way to becoming the largest air force in the world. In May 1940, President Roosevelt's call for 50,000 military aircraft had seemed almost preposterous, but the American aircraft industry had answered the challenge. By September 1941, the Air War Plans Division of the USAAF drew up an interim plan for 59,727 aircraft with an "ultimate" goal of 63,467 aircraft for the USAAF alone.

Chapter Three

Aircraft Factories Go to War

D uring the first two years of the war, the United States remained apart from the hostilities. While President Franklin Roosevelt gave moral support to Britain, most Americans were anxious to remain separate from the bloodshed. However, Roosevelt was well aware of the probability that the United States would eventually be drawn into the war. As they had in World War I, German submarines had begun attacking American ships in the Atlantic. Roosevelt met secretly with British Prime Minister Churchill in August 1941, and the two leaders agreed to work together if the United States was forced into the war.

Meanwhile in Asia, Germany's Axis ally, Japan, continued to expand the empire that it called the Greater East Asia Co-Prosperity Sphere by invading Indochina and the Netherlands East Indies. Roosevelt, increasingly concerned about Japanese aggression, ended exports to the island nation and began to consider further sanctions. Japan viewed these actions as a major impediment to their plans to dominate the Far East and decided to take action. From the Japanese perspective, the only obstacle in the way of a worldwide Axis victory was the U.S. Navy's presence in the Pacific Ocean. Japan planned a single, bold masterstroke to eradicate this threat.

On Sunday morning, December 7, 1941, bombers launched from Japanese aircraft carriers struck at American military installations in Hawaii, particularly the Pearl Harbor Naval Base. The attack was a complete surprise and an immense success. When it ended, more than 2,400 Americans were dead, nearly 200 aircraft were destroyed, and the U.S. Navy's Pacific Fleet was decimated. Eight out of the nine battleships that had been anchored in Pearl Harbor were out of commission.

The following day, President Roosevelt, calling December 7 "a day of infamy," asked Congress for a declaration of war. On December 11, Germany and Italy declared war against the United States and Japan

A technician in Zone 3 at the Douglas Long Beach facility does some fine-tuning in a Plexiglas nose that is destined to be installed in a B-17F heavy bomber. *Alfred Palmer, Office of War Information*

USAAF Manufacturer Site Suffix Codes

During World War II, the U.S. Army Air Forces initiated the practice of assigning each manufacturing plant a two-letter suffix that was attached to the designation of each aircraft manufactured there to identify its source. For example, the Boeing B-17 originated with Boeing's Seattle plant, but some variants, such as the B-17G, were manufactured by a pool of manufacturers. Those built by Boeing in Seattle were designated as B-17G-BO, those built by Douglas in Long Beach were B-17G-DL, and those that Lockheed's Vega component built in Burbank were B-17G-VE. Each individual aircraft carried this information on its data plate in much the same way that automobiles carry a plate with a vehicle identification number (VIN). For the sake of clarity, the suffixes are often omitted when referring to aircraft variants. In this book they are used only when they are important to make a point.

AE	Aeronca	Middletown, OH	DO	Douglas	Santa Monica, CA	NA	North American	Inglewood, CA
BE	Bell	Buffalo, NY	DT	Douglas	Tulsa, OK	NC	North American	Kansas City, MO
BH	Beechcraft	Wichita, KS	FA	Fairchild	Hagerstown, MD	ND	Noorduyn	Montreal, PQ
BL	Bellanca	New Castle, DE	FB	Fairchild	Burlington, NC	NK	NashKelvinator	Detroit, MI
BN	Boeing	Renton, WA	FE	Fleet	Fort Erie, ON	NO	Northrop	Hawthorne, CA
BO	Boeing	Seattle, WA	FL	Fleetwings	Bristol, PA	NT	North American	Dallas, TX
BP	Bureau of Naval Weapons	Washington, DC	FO	Ford	Willow Run, MI	NV	Northrop Ventura	Van Nuys, CA
BS	Bowlus	San Francisco, CA	FR	Frankfort	Frankfort, IN	PI	Piper	Lock Haven, PA
BU	Budd	Philadelphia, PA	GA	G & A Aircraft	Willow Grove, PA	PL	PlattLePage	Eddystone, PA
BW	Boeing	Wichita, KS	GC	General Motors, Fisher Body	Cleveland, OH	RA	Republic	Evansville, IN
BX	Bendix	Detroit, MI	GK	General Motors, Fisher Body	Kansas City, MO	RE	Republic	Farmingdale, NY
CA	Chase	West Trenton, NJ	GM	General Motors, Fisher Body	Detroit, MI	RP	Radioplane	Van Nuys, CA
CE	Cessna	Wichita, KS	GO	Goodyear	Akron, OH	SI	Sikorsky	Stratford, CT
CF	Consolidated	Fort Worth, TX	GR	Grumman	Bethpage, NY	SL	St. Louis	St. Louis, MO
CK	Curtiss	Louisville, KY	HI	Higgins	New Orleans, LA	SP	Spartan	Tulsa, OK
CL	Culver	Wichita, KS	HO	Howard	Chicago, IL	TA	Taylorcraft	Alliance, OH
CN	Chase	Willow Run, MI	HU	Hughes	Culver City, CA	TI	Timm	Van Nuys, CA
CO	Consolidated	San Diego, CA	IN	Interstate	El Segundo, CA	UN	Universal	Bristol, VA
CS	Curtiss	St. Louis, MO	KE	Kellett	Philadelphia, PA	VE	LockheedVega	Burbank, CA
CU	Curtiss	Buffalo, NY	KM	Kaiser	Willow Run, MI	VI	Vickers Canada	Montreal, PQ
CV	Chance Vought	Dallas, TX	LO	Lockheed	Burbank, CA	VN	Vultee	Nashville, TN
DC	Douglas	Chicago, IL	MA	Martin	Baltimore, MD	VU	Vultee	Downey, CA
DE	Douglas	El Segundo, CA	MC	McDonnell	St. Louis, MO	VW	Vultee	Wayne, MI
DK	Douglas	Oklahoma City, OK	MM	McDonnell	Memphis, TN	WO	Waco	Troy, MI
DL	Douglas	Long Beach, CA	MO	Martin	Omaha, NE			

declared war on Britain. The United States was embroiled in World War II, and the American aircraft industry was ready to meet the challenges that lay ahead.

Faced with the Herculean task of managing the largest industrial mobilization in world history, in January 1942 the Roosevelt Administration sought to integrate the civilian and military aspects of the economy through the creation of the War Production Board (WPB). To head this new mobilization agency, Roosevelt tapped Donald Nelson, a former executive with Sears, Roebuck and Company, America's largest retailer. Nelson was faced with reorienting the entire U.S. economy, which meant balancing military requirements with civilian needs, especially those of workers whose efforts underpinned the economy and the war effort.

The armed services wanted the full economy reoriented to the war effort, but Nelson maintained a balance, planning for war production to satisfy most military requirements, while addressing some consumer demands.

In 1942, the WPB developed the Controlled Materials Plan, which allocated strategic materials, such as aluminum, copper, and steel, to specific industrial users. This helped to diminish rivalry among manufacturers. Late in 1942, however, it became apparent that the WPB was unable to fully control the growing war economy because of the

OPPOSITE: Employees of North American Aviation pose with a B-25C at the outdoor final assembly area at the firm's Inglewood, California, flagship plant. *Courtesy Earl Blount*

competing needs and demands of the Army and Navy vis-à-vis civilian production. With this in mind, Roosevelt created the Office of War Mobilization (OWM) in the summer of 1943. Heading the OWM was one of the president's closest advisors, former U.S. Supreme Court Justice James Francis Byrnes. Known as Roosevelt's "assistant president," the new production head soon became one of the most powerful men in Washington.

According to Paul Koistinen, writing in *Arsenal of World War II: The Political Economy of American Warfare*, Byrnes acted "as an arbiter among contending forces in the WPB, settling disputes between the board and the armed services, and dealing with the multiple problems" of the War Manpower Commission, the agency charged with controlling civilian labor markets, and with guaranteeing an unbroken quantity of draftees.

As the OWM ascended, it by no means eclipsed the WPB. Indeed, there would be a whole galaxy of three- and four-letter acronym agencies to deal with production of weapons and war materials during World War II. A full discussion of this complex and interlocking archipelago of Washington bureaucracies is beyond the scope of the present work—and arguably beyond the scope of rational comprehension. With regard to wartime aircraft production, private industry and their millions of workers, not the bureaucrats, were responsible for building the planes.

Among the planemakers, the Glenn Martin Company divided production at its facility near Baltimore between flying boats for the U.S. Navy and medium bombers for the USAAF. Martin's principal production aircraft during World War II was the B-26 Marauder medium bomber, of which production models first reached squadron service in the fall of 1941. Refinements in the design based on combat experience led to the creation of the definitive B-26B variant, of which 1,883 were built at Baltimore through February 1944. In 1942, Martin opened a second Marauder manufacturing facility in the American heartland at Omaha, Nebraska. There, the company would build 1,210 Marauders under the designation B-26C. These aircraft were essentially the same as the later B-26Bs with the larger wings. Martin's last Marauder variants were 300 B-26Fs and 893 B-26Gs, all of them built in Maryland. Martin's principal flying boat type was the remarkable PBM Mariner patrol bomber, which was first delivered in its production form in September 1940. More than 700 of the definitive PBM-3 series rolled out at Baltimore through June 1944, and another 592 PBM-5s were built by the end of 1945.

North of Martin's complex, at Farmingdale on Long Island, Republic Aviation was essentially a one-product company, gearing up to produce vast numbers of its P-47 Thunderbolt fighter, destined to be

U.S. Navy World War II Manufacturer Codes

Whereas the USAAF assigned each manufacturing plant a two-letter suffix that was attached to the designation of each aircraft manufactured to identify its source, the U.S. Navy incorporated a one-letter code into the actual designation itself. While the USAAF codes identified individual plants, the Navy codes identified manufacturers. For example, the Consolidated Catalina was designated as PBY, meaning that it was a "patrol bomber" built by Consolidated (code Y). The second patrol bomber from Consolidated was the PB2Y Coronado. The Grumman Hellcat was designated as F6F, meaning that it was the sixth fighter type ordered from Grumman (code F). Subvariants were designated as F6F-1, F6F-3, and so on. Sometimes manufacturers of different types of aircraft were given the same letter. Some of these letters were assigned to other manufacturers before or after World War II. This list is concerned only with wartime nomenclature.

A	Brewster	H	McDonnell (after 1946)	R	Interstate
B	Boeing	J	North American Aviation	R	Radioplane
C	Curtiss	K	Fairchild	R	Ryan
C	Cessna	K	Kaiser-Fleetwings	S	Sikorsky
D	Douglas	L	Bell	S	Stearman
D	McDonnell (before 1946)	M	Eastern Aircraft (General Motors)	T	Douglas (El Segundo)
E	Piper	M	Martin	T	Northrop
E	Pratt-Read	N	Naval Aircraft Factory	T	Timm
F	Grumman	N	Seversky	U	Chance Vought
G	Goodyear	O	Lockheed	V	Lockheed (Vega component)
G	Eberhart Aeroplane and Motor Company	P	Piper (gliders)	V	Vultee
H	HallAluminum (before 1940)	P	Spartan	W	Waco
H	Howard	R	Aeronca	Y	Consolidated

PBM-1 Mariner flying boats are seen here on the factory floor of the Glenn Martin Company facility near Baltimore. The Mariner was in production before the United States entered World War II. It also had a long postwar career. *Glen L. Martin Company*

The forward fuselage of a B-26B Marauder. The Glenn Martin Company built 1,883 B-26Bs at its Maryland factory. *Glen L. Martin Company*

one of the USAAF's foremost warplanes. Republic had originated in 1931 as the Seversky Aircraft Corporation, founded by Alexander de Seversky, a World War I fighter ace with Tsar Nicholas II's navy. He was sent to the United States as air attaché in 1917, and when the Russian Revolution occurred he decided to stay. Despite these small military contracts, the company was never profitable, so Seversky's investors voted him out in 1939 and reorganized as Republic Aviation. The reorganized company developed a series of fighter aircraft that included the P-43 Lancer and culminated with the P-47, which debuted in 1941. After a handful of P-43s that were delivered through March 1942, a total of 15,231 P-47 Thunderbolts were essentially the only product built by Republic during the war. To support the large number orders that were placed for P-47s, Republic opened a second production facility at Evansville, Indiana.

A few miles from Republic, the Grumman "Iron Works" at Bethpage, Long Island, would be synonymous with U.S. naval aviation for 40 of aviation's first 70 years. This reputation was solidly grounded in the line of radial-engine fighters built beginning in the early 1930s. By World War II, this line included the F4F Wildcat that entered service early in 1940 with the U.S. Navy and with the British Royal Navy and Royal Air Force, which designated it as the Martlet. When the United States entered World War II, the F4F Wildcat was the Navy's standard carrier-based fighter. It was also in service with U.S. Marine Corps units in the Southwest Pacific Theater.

The process of designing the Wildcat's successor, the F6F Hellcat, was underway at the Iron Works as the United States entered the war, and the first flight of the prototype occurred in June 1942. Production aircraft were first delivered at the end of 1942, and by the end of 1943, more than 2,500 Hellcats had been delivered, allowing the U.S. Navy to equip every fighter squadron on its entire "fast carrier" force with F6Fs. The definitive Hellcat was probably the F6F-5, which first flew in April 1944. Of a total of more than 12,000 Hellcats built, more than 7,800 were F6F-5s. Second only to the Hellcat among Grumman products during World War II was the TBF Avenger, the U.S. Navy's principal torpedo bomber from mid-1942 through the end of the war. It was ordered into limited production in December 1940, although the prototype would not make its first flight for eight months. The Iron Works delivered the first production series Avengers a month after Pearl Harbor.

continued on page 59

LEFT: Working on a radial engine nacelle at the Glenn Martin Company factory, November 1943. *Glen L. Martin Company*

OPPOSITE: A Block 50 B-26B Marauder nears completion at the Glenn Martin Company factory in late 1943. The final two blocks of B-26B production were the variant's largest, with 400 units between them. *Glen L. Martin Company*

A mysterious stranger stands on the runway at Farmingdale on Long Island to contemplate a Block 15 Republic P-47D Thunderbolt. Beginning with Block 25 in 1944, the P-47Ds had a bubble canopy. *Author collection*

5 Grand

Boeing celebrated the 5,000th B-17 Flying Fortress manufactured in Seattle by allowing everyone at the plant an opportunity to sign this Block 70 B-17G (tail number 43-37716) as it passed their station along the assembly line. An estimated 35,000 "autographs" decorated the aircraft, appropriately nicknamed *5 Grand*. The delivery to the USAAF in May 1944 was a national media event, and Seattle native Edward Unger was selected as her pilot. In turn, he picked an all-Seattle crew. Going overseas, he discovered that the signatures created so much drag on the plane that her air speed was about 7 miles per hour slower than other B-17Gs. Though the Luftwaffe made a concerted effort to shoot *5 Grand* down, she completed 78 missions with several crews and assignments with both the 96th and 388th Bombardment Groups. She returned to Seattle in June 1945 as part of a War Bond tour with many of the signatures still present. There was talk of her finding a home at a museum in Seattle, but funds were unavailable and she was scrapped in Kingman, Arizona, in 1946 or 1947.

The 5,000th B-17 Flying Fortress manufactured in Seattle after Pearl Harbor poses on the ramp at Boeing Field with some of the workers who helped to build her. *Boeing Archives*

continued from page 54

A total of 2,290 TBF-1 series Avengers rolled out at Bethpage through the end of 1943.

The U.S. Navy was so eager for the Hellcat that it sought alternate means of producing the other Iron Works products, turning to the world's largest industrial company: General Motors. GM set up its Eastern Aircraft Division and converted its Linden, New Jersey, facility to build Wildcats under the FM designation; its Trenton, New Jersey, plant would build Avengers under the TBM designation. GM built 1,150 FM-1s, of which 311 were transferred to the United Kingdom under lend-lease as the Martlet V (later the Wildcat V). This number was dwarfed by 4,777 FM-2s, of which the British were lend-leased 340 as Wildcat VI. The Eastern Aircraft Division also rolled out 2,882 TBM-1s and 4,661 TBM-3s through September 1945.

Another East Coast planemaker that emerged as a prominent supplier to the U.S. Navy during World War II was Chance Vought of Stratford, Connecticut. Tracing its lineage back to 1917, the company had been part of Bill Boeing's 1929 industry mega-merger that created United Aircraft & Transport Corporation (UATC). Vought's claim to fame during the war would be its F4U Corsair fighter. Created by Chief Engineer Rex Beisel, the Corsair was designed around the new Pratt & Whitney XR-2800-4 Double Wasp engine that delivered 1,850 horsepower. On the Double Wasp, Vought hung a huge propeller with a diameter of 13 feet, 4 inches, which required designing the Corsair with its distinctive gull wings that make it instantly recognizable. The XF4U-1 Corsair made its first flight in May 1940, but the first production contract was not issued for more than a year. It was 1942 before the first production F4U-1 aircraft was delivered. Initial carrier tests were not promising, so the Navy decided to earmark them for delivery to U.S. Marine Corps units in the Southwest Pacific Theater. The plane was a success there, with top Marine Corps aces, such as Gregory "Pappy" Boyington, flying the Corsair.

While 4,699 production-series F4U-1s were built by Vought, two other manufacturers also were involved in production. The Goodyear Aircraft Corporation (a division of the rubber company) manufactured 4,006 in Akron, Ohio, under the designation FG-1. (In the field

RIGHT: Ruby Reed and Merle Judd at work inside the fuselage of an F6F Hellcat fighter at the legendary Grumman Iron Works on Long Island. *Office of War Information*

OPPOSITE: Avenger torpedo bombers, designed by Grumman under the TBF designation, roll off the General Motors Eastern Aircraft Division assembly line in Trenton, New Jersey, under the TBM designation. Eastern built 7,543 TBMs, compared to Grumman's 2,290 production series TBFs. *Author collection*

The big Goodyear facility in Akron, Ohio, was established to manufacture Goodyear's famous blimps, but during World War II the complex was pressed into service to make Vought-designed Corsair fighter planes. *Author collection*

OPPOSITE: A Vought F4U-1 Corsair is tested in the huge wind tunnel at the Langley Research Center in Hampton, Virginia. Then owned by the National Advisory Committee for Aeronautics (NACA), the wind tunnel was part of the government's efforts to aid the American aircraft industry. It is still used by NACA's successor organization, the National Aeronautics and Space Administration (NASA). The Corsair was a top U.S. Navy fighter during World War II. *NASA photo*

of aviation, Goodyear was best known for lighter-than-air blimps that it manufactured for the U.S. Navy and other customers.)

By December 1941, Boeing had delivered about 150 B-17C and B-17D Flying Fortress heavy bombers to the USAAF. As early as 1940, it had become evident that a major flaw in the original Flying Fortress was a lack of defensive armament in the tail. Guns bristled from its nose, waist, and belly, but it was a six-sided fortress with no guns on its most vulnerable side. Boeing responded with the B-17E (Model 299-O),

which had the tail turret that would be standard in the rest of the production series. The B-17E was also the first Flying Fortress produced in large numbers—512 were built, all at Boeing's Plant 2 in Seattle—and the first to see combat on a regular basis. B-17Es were deployed to Australia in early 1942, and in July 1942 they arrived in England to become the nucleus of the USAAF Eighth Air Force that would undertake the great strategic offensive against Germany. The B-17F (Model 299P) was

continued on page 64

A mass of B-17F Flying Fortresses moves toward completion on the factory floor at Boeing's Plant 2 in Seattle. *Boeing Archives*

Making its first "flight" thanks to a huge factory crane, the fuselage for a future B-17F moves out to be joined with its wings. *Boeing Archives*

RIGHT: A group of technicians at Boeing's Plant 2 study a detail issue in the aft fuselage/tail section destined to be incorporated into a B-17 Flying Fortress. *Boeing Archives*

OPPOSITE: Boeing employees inside an aft fuselage/tail section of a B-17 Flying Fortress. *Boeing Archives*

continued from page 60

introduced in April 1942 with more powerful engines, a ventral ball turret, and a one-piece, Plexiglas nose.

Because of the importance of the B-17, the USAAF decided during the summer of 1941 that multiple manufacturers should build the aircraft. Plans were made to have some of the production of B-17Es and later variants taken over by companies with surplus capacity, but the B-17F soon superseded the B-17E, and the plan was implemented with the later variant instead.

Douglas and Lockheed's Vega subsidiary was brought into the pool and a coordinating committee known as the Boeing-Douglas-Vega (BDV) Committee was formed. It was an unprecedented system that would be used later in World War II and once after World War II (with

the Boeing B-47). It was a prototype for similar cooperation on the B-24, the B-29, and other programs, and it proved an example of former—and future—competitors working together for a common war effort. Of course, during World War II, there was no shortage of work for the planemakers. Under the arrangement, Douglas and Vega were not subcontractors to Boeing but were contracted directly by the USAAF, with Boeing acting as the prime design contractor. Eventually, the BDV Committee became a large and amazingly well managed production organization, with regular meetings and designated subcommittees.

Over the course of the 15 months the B-17F was in production, 605 B-17F-DLs were built by Douglas and another 500 B-17F-VEs by Lockheed's Vega subsidiary—all in Southern California. Meanwhile, Boeing's Plant 2 rolled out a staggering 2,300 B-17F-BOs. Ironically,

A trio of Boeing employees carefully install the nose of a B-17F Flying Fortress. This meticulous task was repeated dozens of times each week during World War II. Soon, a USAAF bombardier would be looking down at Hitler's Third Reich from this Plexiglas perch. *Boeing Archives*

even as Douglas was building B-17F-DLs at its Long Beach factory, Boeing was building Douglas-designed A-20C-BOs at Plant 2.

As huge as the B-17F numbers were by prewar standards, they were dwarfed by production totals of the B-17G. Introduced in the autumn of 1943, the B-17G (Model 299P) has often and correctly been described as the definitive Flying Fortress. It had the ball turret, the R1820-97 engines, and all of the other B-17F improvements, as well as a forward-firing Bendix "chin" turret that made it a true Flying Fortress. It also typically carried a bomb load of 6,000 to 9,600 pounds. Again, the BDV Committee partners were called upon to supplement Boeing production. The California companies Douglas and Vega produced 2,395 and 2,250, respectively, and 4,035 were built in Seattle.

In the year after Pearl Harbor, Southern California's role in the American aviation industry grew like that of no other region in the United States. The Southland, as locals called it, was certainly the Detroit of aircraft manufacturing.

RIGHT: Many American workers found it patriotic to "give up a holiday to speed victory." This look inside the Boeing factory just five days before Christmas 1943 shows the wing-join area of the floor. The propellers have just been hung and the wingtips have already been painted for purposes of correct balance as the major assembly of each B-17G Flying Fortress takes place. *Boeing Archives*

OPPOSITE: Seen at Boeing Plant 2, this B-17G Flying Fortress is about to have its wings joined. The guns have been installed in the top turret, but the Plexiglas cover is still lying on the wing near the number-three engine nacelle. *Boeing Archives*

Marvin Miles, the aviation editor of the *Los Angeles Times* wrote enthusiastically, "Southern California aircraft plants rolled up their sleeves and waded into the gigantic production task, rapidly turning the Southland into the plane capital of the world." Indeed, it was not hyperbole, given that by the end of 1943, American production was more than double that of any other country.

The Southland manufacturers—Consolidated, Douglas, Lockheed, North American, Northrop, and others—shared inventions, technical information, and materials through their Aircraft War Production Council. This involved 10,000 material exchanges and 1,500 technical reports in 1942 alone. As with the American aircraft industry in general, Southland manufacturers evolved faster production methods, enlarged factories, built new plants, combed the country for technicians, and started new training schools. Women were hired by the thousands. From a negligible proportion, they became 35 percent of the total aviation workforce in the Southland by the beginning of 1943.

By this time, the major companies in Southern California had reached a combined annual production rate of more than $2 billion

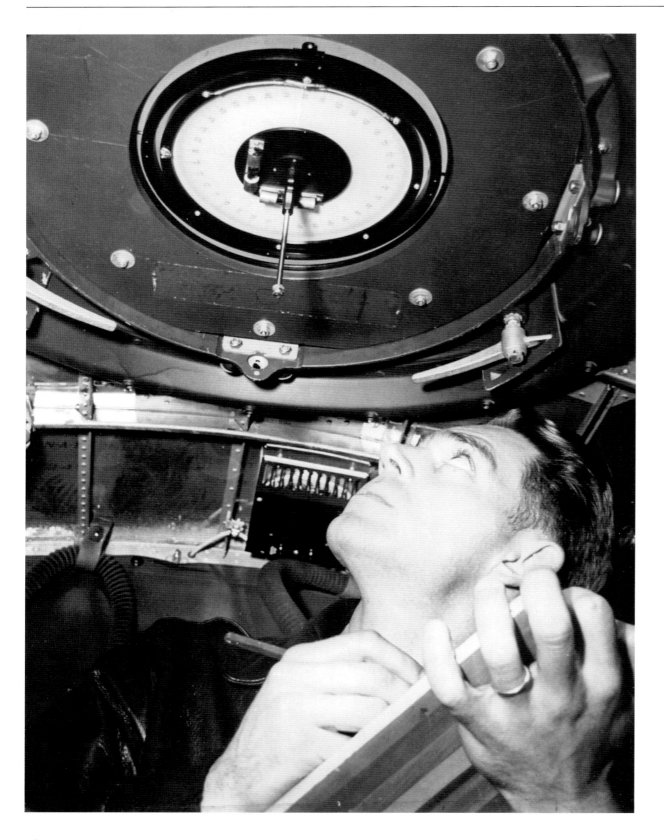

(approximately $22.5 billion in current dollars) and were building about 60 percent of the nation's gross weight in airframes. During World War II, Consolidated, Douglas, and North American were the three largest American aircraft manufacturers, reckoned by the total number of airframes produced. They were also all in the top four in terms of airframe pounds. Boeing was third in airframe pounds and fifth in total airframes. Curtiss was fourth in the later comparison.

So rapidly did the industry expand that by December 7, 1942, the Los Angeles Chamber of Commerce aviation department estimated that approximately a third of the population of Los Angeles County was dependent on aviation. While the household names accounted for the lion's share of the huge numbers of employees and airframe pounds, nearly a thousand firms listed and classified by the chamber as aircraft subcontractors, accessory and parts manufacturers, and other suppliers, were also vital to the effort.

One often overlooked advantage that the Southern California factories had over their counterparts in more northerly climes—including Britain and Germany—was the weather. Because of the almost continuous warm and sunny weather, much of the final assembly work could be done outdoors most of the year. This gave the planemakers in the Southland a large increase in factory floor space for the cost of canvas used as portable "nose hangars" and other light equipment. The Southern California weather came to be referred to as one of the American aircraft industry's "secret weapons."

If there was one individual who stood out among the Southland's captains of industry, it was Donald Wills Douglas. The man who had made his mark before the war with the DC-3, was, in a word, the "man." In 1941, *Fortune* magazine wrote, "The development of the airplane in the days between the wars is the greatest engineering story there ever was, and in the heart of it is Donald Douglas."

Courted by politicians and often in the company of Hollywood stars and starlets, Douglas lived in a large, movie-mogul-worthy mansion in the 1400 block of San Vicente Boulevard in Santa Monica. He operated three huge factories in the area—at Santa Monica, El

continued on page 74

LEFT: A Boeing Shadow Compass is installed in a B-17G on June 14, 1944. According to the press release that accompanied this photograph when it was circulated for publication, "scientists made the greatest improvement to the magnetic compass in 4,000 years" by applying the "age-old theory of the sundial." *Boeing Archives*

RIGHT: Though this Flying Fortress has reached the point of major assembly where all the big parts come together, there is still a great deal of detail work to be done in the fuselage. Note the ocean of forward fuselages in the background. *Boeing Archives*

AIRCRAFT FACTORIES GO TO WAR

LEFT: Workers at the Douglas Long Beach factory do interior work near what will be the waist-gun positions within the fuselage of a B-17F. Douglas built the Boeing-designed bombers as part of the Boeing-Douglas-Vega (BDV) committee that pooled production resources. *Alfred Palmer, Office of War Information*

BELOW: Donald Douglas wielded the shovel at the groundbreaking for his new Long Beach factory complex in November 1940. Standing behind him are George Strompl of Douglas Aircraft, Captain R. B. Coffman of the U.S. Navy, and General George Brett of the U.S. Army. Both services would operate aircraft built here. *Courtesy Harry Gann*

THE AMERICAN AIRCRAFT FACTORY IN WORLD WAR II

California Governor Earl Warren smiles approvingly as Don Douglas cracks a joke. Previously, Warren had served as state attorney general. Elected governor in 1942, he was named to the United States Supreme Court in 1953. Flanking the industrialist and politician in the Douglas cafeteria are Ted Conent (left) and A. M. Rochlen. *Courtesy Harry Gann*

continued from page 70

Segundo, and Long Beach. Between 1940 and 1943, the Douglas workforce increased from 8,000 to 160,000, accounting for just more than half of the Southland's total aircraft industry employment of 300,000. Major Douglas products included attack bombers for both the U.S. Navy and the USAAF, and more than 10,000 military DC-3 airliners delivered mainly under the USAAF designation C-47. Douglas was also a member of the Boeing-Douglas-Vega Committee, the pool of manufacturers that built Boeing B-17s.

When the war began, the flagship Douglas factory was at Santa Monica, where Don Douglas had been building planes for two decades. Among the most important of the new factories in the Southland was the Douglas facility at Long Beach, which had opened its doors late in 1941, just before Pearl Harbor. The Long Beach plant, the company's third, was designed to be its largest and would produce nearly 10,000 aircraft during World War II (a third of the Douglas total), including C-47s, B-17s, A-20s, and A-26s. After World War II, Long Beach became the site of the corporate headquarters and was where all Douglas jetliners would be built. The Long Beach factory was still going strong when Douglas merged with McDonnell in 1967 and when McDonnell Douglas was absorbed by Boeing in 1997.

As noted in Chapter 2, Don Douglas had taken a 51 percent share when Jack Northrop opened his reconstituted Northrop Corporation at El Segundo in 1932. In turn, the El Segundo operation became a division of Douglas Aircraft in 1938, when Jack Northrop left to put together a syndicate of investors to start yet another new company. In 1939, Jack moved less than 10 miles down the road to Hawthorne, California, and started Northrop Aircraft, Inc.

When Northrop left Douglas, Don Douglas integrated the Northrop production line into his Douglas operations as the Douglas El Segundo division. Northrop was producing a series of military aircraft, including sturdy, low-winged, single-engine attack bombers. Among these were the U.S. Army Air Corps A-13 (Northrop Model 2C) and A-17 (Northrop Model 8) series.

While Northrop moved on when Douglas absorbed El Segundo, his key designer, Ed Heinemann, stayed. Through World War II and the two decades that followed, Heinemann earned a well-deserved place in the pantheon of the greatest designers to work in the American aviation industry.

Heinemann's first project after the plant officially became Douglas El Segundo in 1938 was to create a fast, twin-engine attack aircraft in response to a request for proposals issued by the U.S. Army Air Corps. The DB-7 was first flown in 1938, powered by a pair of Pratt & Whitney R1830 Wasps. Though the DB-7 would earn a United States production contract eventually, the first sales were export contracts. France and Belgium both placed orders in early 1939, and approximately 64 airplanes (of 270 ordered) were delivered to France during the early months of World War II. However, these aircraft did not see combat until a few weeks before Germany defeated France in June 1940.

During the summer of 1940, undelivered aircraft on French and Belgian orders placed with many American manufacturers were diverted to Britain's Royal Air Force. Remaining French and Belgian DB-7s went to the RAF under the designation Boston Mk I. The first round of orders from the U.S. Army Air Corps came in June 1940, calling for 143 aircraft under the designation A-20A and 63 as A-20s. The given name for the American aircraft would be the Havoc rather than Boston. In October, 999 A-20Bs with improved Cyclone engines, self-sealing fuel tanks, and upgraded armament were added to the order books.

Whereas most of the earlier aircraft were manufactured mainly in Santa Monica, the A-20Bs would be manufactured at the new Douglas plant in Long Beach. As previously noted, the A-20C series would be manufactured by Douglas at Santa Monica and by Boeing at Plant 2 in Seattle while Douglas was building Boeing B-17s at Long Beach.

The next Havoc production variants, the A-20G and A-20H, were distinguished from earlier types by having solid noses rather than the transparent "bombardier" noses of earlier types. The nose contained a

continued on page 78

The main entrance to the Douglas Long Beach plant, completed in 1941, was extremely futuristic and "Forties Modern." The globe was a three-dimensional representation of the Douglas logo, which celebrated the Douglas airplanes that made history's first round-the-world flight in 1924. *Courtesy Harry Gann*

LEFT: A color view of the Douglas SBD Dauntless line at El Segundo plant. The briefly used red outline on the insignia dates the scene to the middle of 1943. *Courtesy Harry Gann*

OPPOSITE: SBD Dauntless dive bombers destined for the carriers of the U.S. Navy dominated the assembly line at the Douglas El Segundo plant in February 1943. *Courtesy Harry Gann*

A group of workers at the Douglas Santa Monica facility clown for the photographer with the propeller of a P-70. By 1943, such aircraft had starters that eliminated the need to crank the prop. The P-70 was the night fighter variant of the A-20 attack bomber, of which Douglas built about 6,000 at Santa Monica. Only 60 P-70s were built. *Courtesy Harry Gann*

continued from page 74

variety of forward-firing armament, including four 20mm cannons plus machine guns. Another solid-nosed, heavily armed derivative was the P-70 Havoc night fighter. It carried no bombs and was equipped with search radar and a powerful "turbinlight" searchlight that was turned on when the Havoc got close to its target. The final two production variants, the A-20J and the A-20K, returned to the transparent nose, but it was a frameless, blown Plexiglas nose rather than the faceted nose of early Havocs.

The DB-7/A-20 family was produced in greater numbers than any other Douglas warplane. Company records show that 7,477 were built, including 999 A-20A-DLs built in Long Beach, 808 A-20C-DOs built in Santa Monica, and 2,850 A-20G-DOs, also built in Santa Monica.

During World War II, Douglas would use El Segundo mainly for the SBD Dauntless, the U.S. Navy's most important carrier-based bomber of World War II. It served for the entire duration of American involvement in the war and is credited with sinking more enemy tonnage in the Pacific Theater than any other aircraft type (and possibly more tonnage than any single type of surface ship).

The lineage of the Douglas Dauntless can be traced through the

A color view of A-20 Havocs on the Douglas assembly line at Santa Monica in 1942 before the red spot was removed from the national insignia. *Courtesy Harry Gann*

family tree of the El Segundo plant. The ancestor of the Dauntless was the Northrop BT-1 basic trainer, designed by Ed Heinemann and first flown at El Segundo in August 1935. First ordered in 1939, the SBD was to be a dive bomber based on the earlier airframe design. The dive bomber was a type that was conceived in the 1930s and used extensively in the early years of World War II, especially the German Ju.87 Stuka. While other attack planes, such as torpedo bombers, released their bombs in level flight, a dive bomber aimed its ordnance while hurtling toward the target in a near-vertical plunge, releasing the bombs while pulling out of the dive using large flaps known as dive brakes. In order to reduce buffet in a steep dive, and to reduce stress on the airframe, Ed Heinemann designed perforated dive brakes that came to be known as "Swiss cheese flaps."

The Dauntless made its first flight in May 1940, though production deliveries did not begin until early 1941. Deliveries of the improved SBD-3 began in September 1940 and the type was present on all American carriers at the time the United States entered World War II. Douglas would deliver 584 SBD-3s for the U.S. Navy and an additional 168 to the USAAF under the designation A-24. In October 1942, deliveries began of the further improved SBD-4 type. Of these, 780 SBD-4s were delivered to the U.S. Navy and 170 A-24As went to the USAAF. All were built at El Segundo. Like the SBD-4, but powered by a Wright R1820-60 engine, the SBD-5 began to roll out in February 1943. There would be 2,965 SBD-4s for the U.S. Navy, 615 A-24Bs for the USAAF, and 60 SBD-5As delivered to the U.S. Marine Corps. With this series, production shifted from California to Tulsa, Oklahoma. The final Dauntless variant was the SBD-6, of which 450 were made. It was like the previous types but powered with a Wright R1820-60 engine.

Dauntlesses served on practically every American carrier in the Pacific, fought in every battle where carrier air power played a role, and sunk numerous enemy ships, including six Japanese carriers and a battleship. The Dauntless also had a heroic career with the U.S. Marine Corps and with the USAAF. Ultimately, 5,936 SBDs and A-24s were produced.

In addition to the three Southern California factories, Douglas opened and operated three out-of-state factories in areas deep within the continent. The Oklahoma City factory was designed specifically to provide Douglas with a second production line to build C-47 transports. The factory in Tulsa, Oklahoma, built USAAF attack bombers and was also used by Douglas when it was brought into the production pool for Consolidated B-24 Liberators.

continued on page 84

This drawing illustrated the Douglas Santa Monica "Flow-line" assembly line as it appeared in 1943 when it rivaled Willow Run as the longest airplane assembly line in the world. The line was located in a building that was 700 feet long, but a series of switchbacks gave it a total length of 6,100 feet. Both main and subassembly lines were mounted on traveling tubular jigs that were synchronized to the same production speed and coordinated through a central control panel in the office of the plant manager. The result was a mile-long parade of moving jigs on which fuselage half shells were fabricated, interior installations were made, and the half shells were finally mated. Inner wings, traveling on overhead conveyors at synchronized speeds, moved on tracks to appointed junctures with the main line. Completed aircraft sections flowed in a stream past their builders. Stockrooms and racks built into line positions were fed and replenished by overhead monorail conveyors. The Flow-line utilized the slope in the factory floor through the last 800 feet of pre-flight travel. The finished aircraft then proceeded through final inspections via gravity and their own landing gear. *Author collection*

FACE

A Douglas employee checks the aft gun in an A-20 Havoc on the flight line at Santa Monica. *Courtesy Harry Gann*

Engine mechanics are trained in the technical nuances of the Pratt & Whitney R1830 Twin Wasp radial aircraft engine, circa 1942. Such engines powered myriad World War II aircraft, including the Consolidated B-24 Liberator and the Douglas C-47 Skytrain. *Alfred Palmer, Office of War Information*

RIGHT: The C-47 assembly line was just one of several that were operating simultaneously at the sprawling Douglas complex in Long Beach. *Courtesy Harry Gann*

OPPOSITE: At work near the wheel well of a bomber at the Douglas Long Beach factory. *Alfred Palmer, Office of War Information*

continued from page 80

Finally, in 1942 and 1943, Douglas constructed a 2-million-square-foot factory at Orchard Place on the outskirts of Chicago to build USAAF C-54 transports, the military version of the commercial DC-4. The idea was that a Chicago site would take advantage of the huge workforce and unrivaled rail hub of the nation's then second-largest city.

During the middle years of World War II, Douglas was the Southland's industrial powerhouse. The July 5, 1943, issue of *Time* magazine reported:

During the month of May Douglas Aircraft Co. produced 13,096,000 pounds of combat and cargo planes—more than one-fifth (by weight)

of the output of the entire industry. That figure was one and a half times the Douglas production rate a year ago. Thirteen million pounds of aircraft would equal more than 2,000 individual planes of the average weight (6,400 pounds) produced so far this year, or more than 200 huge transports like Douglas' new DC-4 (which weighs 32 tons loaded). But dark, saturnine Donald Wills Douglas (whose friends say "his rare moments of elation correspond to the ordinary man's mild depressions") is nowhere near through making production records. His three big new Eastern plants will not be in full production 'til midsummer, and last week he announced the lease of still another huge factory: at the request of the Army, next month Douglas will take over General Motors' Los Angeles tank plant.

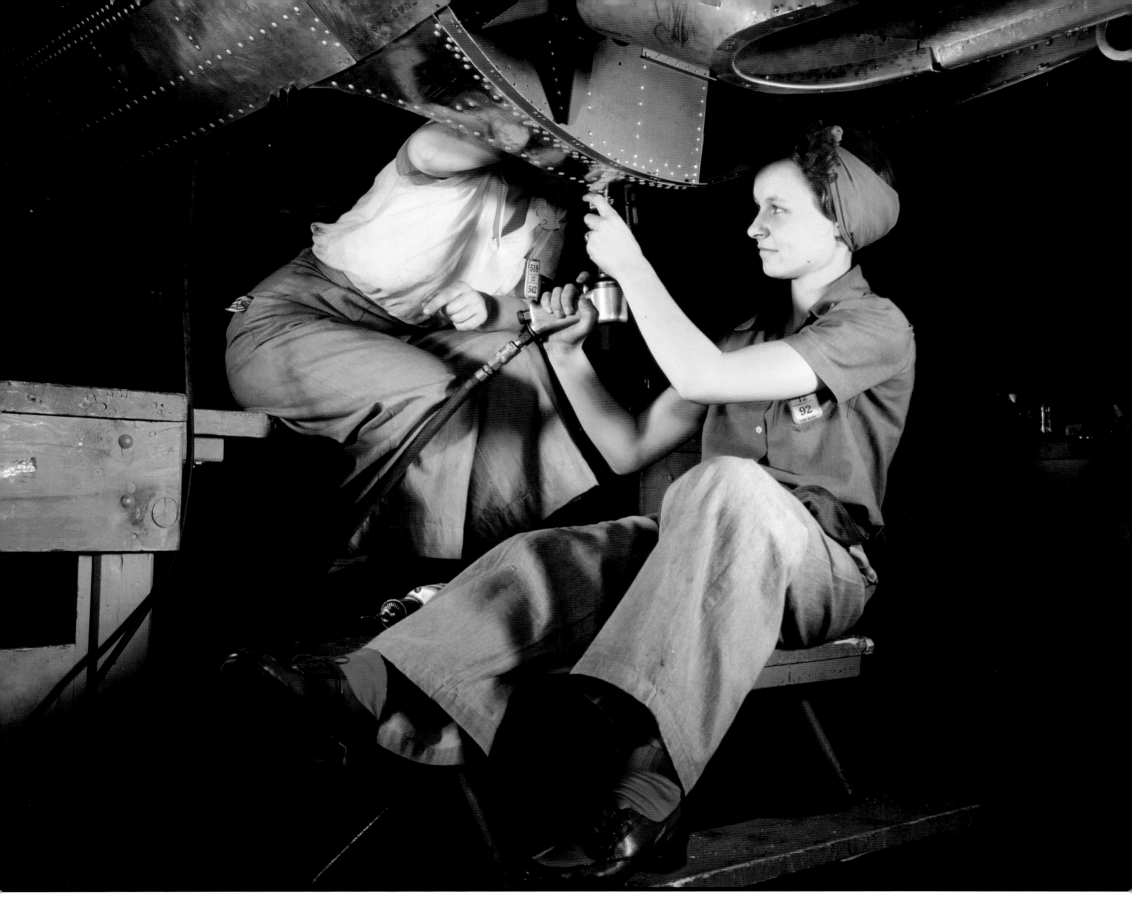

Built in Connecticut, New York, or Illinois, these Pratt & Whitney R1830 Twin Wasp radial engines were shipped to California to become parts of the C-47s in the background. These two dozen Twin Wasps are among more than 173,000 that were built between 1932 and 1951, the lion's share of them between 1942 and 1945.
Courtesy Harry Gann

In Inglewood, just across Sepulveda Boulevard from El Segundo, North American Aviation was rapidly moving to eclipse Douglas as America's biggest planemaker. As the war began for the United States in 1941, the foremost products of North American Aviation were military training aircraft. By that time, the company's Yale family of trainers had been marketed to the governments of France, Peru, and Thailand, as well as Britain and the United States. With more than 1,500 aircraft built, the Yale program was an extraordinary first aircraft for North American Aviation. It established the company as one of the most important new planemakers in the United States on the eve of World War II and paved the way for the development of the legendary AT-6 Texan, which first flew in September 1938 and was first delivered to the U.S. Army early in 1940.

The AT-6 Texan has been called "the most universally used plane in history" and, while that may be an exaggeration, she is certainly the most universally used trainer ever built. With the possible exception of the Soviet Polikarpov Po-2, the Texan series tallied the largest production totals—15,495 by company records—of any trainer in history. Most of these were delivered during 1942. Many of the Texans delivered under USAAF contracts were diverted to the U.S. Navy under the designation SNJ.

Midway through the AT-6A program, production demands on the North American Aviation Inglewood plant became so great that a sprawling new factory complex was built near Dallas, Texas. Eventually, 1,330 of the AT-6As and all of the 7,758 AT-6B through AT-6D Texans, as well as a large number of other North American Aviation aircraft, would be built in the Dallas plant.

The crew that made it possible pose with the 2,000th Douglas C-47 produced at Long Beach. The USAAF officially reckons that Douglas went on to build 4,285 C-47s here during World War II. More were built in Oklahoma City. *Courtesy Harry Gann*

North American's first venture into twin-engined military aircraft had been its Model NA-21, ordered by the U.S. Army Air Corps under the conveniently coincidental designation XB-21. Nicknamed Dragon, it first flew in December 1936 and was evaluated opposite the Boeing XB-17 and the Douglas XB-18. Of the three, the XB-21 did not win a production contract.

Dutch Kindelberger did not, however, lose faith in the idea that North American should build a twin-engine bomber. The next step was a twin-engined, twin-tailed medium bomber, which North American Aviation developed as the NA-40. Produced during 1938, the NA-40 prototype made its first flight in February 1939. Smaller and trimmer than the XB-21, the new aircraft attracted a good deal of interest within the Air Corps. In September 1939, an order was received for 184 NA-62 production aircraft under the designation B-25.

Built in Inglewood, the first 24 B-25s—named Mitchell after air-power advocate General Billy Mitchell—were delivered by September 1940, at which time the Air Corps ordered the remainder to be built under the designation B-25A with increased armor and newly developed self-sealing fuel tanks. Forty of these aircraft were built as the NA-62A and delivered as B-25As between May and August 1941. The

specifications were again changed, this time to a B-25B standard that involved replacing fixed 30mm machine guns with power turrets that had .50-caliber guns. The modest number of B-25Bs was followed by a major order for 1,625 B-25Cs that began to roll out of North American's Inglewood plant in January 1942, just a month after the United States entered World War II.

It was obvious that meeting the USAAF's projected need for Mitchells would overload the capacity of North American's California production capability, so a new factory, designated with the manufacturer's code NC, was built in Kansas City, Kansas. The planes constructed at this plant, beginning in February 1942, were designated B-25D, although they were virtually identical to the Inglewood-built B-25Cs except for modified exhaust outlets. There were 2,290 Kansas City B-25D-NCs, compared to 1,625 Inglewood B-25C-NAs.

The Mitchells' speed, maneuverability, and ability to fly at a very low level made them very potent weapons when used to attack enemy ground targets. In January 1943, North American Aviation converted five B-25Cs to carry a nose-mounted 75mm howitzer, one of the largest guns yet carried by an operational American warplane. This led to an order for 400 Inglewood-built B-25G-NAs with the howitzer as standard

RIGHT: Lieutenant Mike Hunter was a USAAF pilot assigned to the Douglas Aircraft Company to evaluate and accept warplanes as they came off the line. He poses here with an A-20 Havoc. *Alfred Palmer, Office of War Information*

OPPOSITE: A veritable sea of North American Aviation training aircraft is shown outside the Inglewood, California, plant. The British Empire acquired these aircraft under the name "Harvard"—to the USAAF they were known as the AT-6 Texan. *Boeing Archives*

A North American employee does some touchup work on a Texan under the warm California sun. *Courtesy Earl Blount*

Members of the experimental staff at the North American Aviation plant in Inglewood, California, observe wind tunnel tests on a scale model of a North American B-25 Mitchell bomber. *Alfred Palmer, Office of War Information*

equipment. In August 1943, the USAAF ordered 1,000 B-25H-NAs with the 75mm gun augmented by four nose-mounted and four side-mounted forward-firing .50-caliber machine guns, as well as a top turret, two waist guns, and a tail turret. The U.S. Navy also ordered 248 of these to be delivered to the Marine Corps as the PBJ-1H.

The final model in the Mitchell family was North American Aviation's NA-108, which the USAAF designated B-25J. With a glazed bombardier's compartment in the nose, the B-25J was the successor to the B-25D and could carry up to 6,746 pounds of ordnance. More B-25Js were built than any other subvariant: 4,318 were delivered to the USAAF, 255 to the U.S. Navy as PBJ-1J, and 316 to the RAF as Mitchell Mk III. While the B-25H assembly line at Inglewood wound down in July 1944, the B-25J remained in production at Kansas City until the end of the war.

A few moments' flying time north of the Hollywood Hills from the Douglas and North American Aviation Southland operations,

Lockheed and its Lockheed-Vega subsidiary were rapidly expanding in the hangars and factory buildings surrounding the Burbank Airport. The Vega plant concentrated mainly on Lockheed's contribution to the multifactory pool, building Boeing B-17s and Consolidated B-24s, while the main Lockheed plant built mostly aircraft of Lockheed design. The biggest Lockheed product of World War II was one of the USAAF's most memorable fighters: the unique twin-engine P-38 Lightning. Designed by Kelly Johnson as Lockheed Model 22, the fighter was probably the best such machine produced by American industry in years leading up to World War II. It was the first production airplane faster than 400 miles per hour, and it would be used by the top USAAF aces in World War II.

The P-38 program began in June 1937 after Lockheed won the competition for a U.S. Army Air Corps contract to build a high-speed, twin-engine air superiority fighter. Hall Hibbard and Kelly Johnson gave the Model 22 an unusual twin fuselage to accommodate its powerplant. Said

RIGHT: Former child star Joe Cobb spent most of World War II building B-25 bombers at Inglewood. He was just five years old in 1921 when his father sent him to audition for producer Hal Roach's comedy series that became *Our Gang*. He appeared in more than 90 shorts through 1929, but in fewer than ten films thereafter. His last appearance was an uncredited role in the 1944 Judy Garland picture *Meet Me in St. Louis*. *Franklin D. Roosevelt Library*

FAR RIGHT: James Howard "Dutch" Kindelberger was the hardworking entrepreneur who turned North American Aviation from a forgettable paper-holding company into one of the largest planemakers in world history. During World War II, his company built 41,839 aircraft, more than any other American company. Second-place Consolidated-Vultee built just 74 percent as many. During the war, Kindelberger lived in a sprawling gated property in the 500 block of North Cliffwood Avenue in the Brentwood Heights area of Los Angeles, a short drive up Sepulveda Boulevard from the factory at Inglewood. *Author collection*

OPPOSITE: A woman works on a Wright R2600 Cyclone radial airplane motor at the North American Aviation plant in Inglewood. *Alfred Palmer, Office of War Information*

Johnson, "It was considered a radically different design—even funny looking, some said. It wasn't to me. There was a reason for everything that went into it, a logical evolution. The shape took care of itself. In design, you are forced to develop unusual solutions to unusual problems."

The first XP-38 prototype was secretly constructed at Burbank between June and December 1938, first flown in January 1939, and first flown all the way across the United States three weeks later. The Air Corps placed orders for 13 service-test aircraft under the designation YP-38, and when World War II began in Europe in September 1939 an additional 20 upgraded YP-38s under the simple designation P-38.

More than 1,800 Lightning fighters were delivered to the USAAF under the designations P-38, P-38D, P-38E, P-38F, and P-38G. These were complemented by 300 Lightning photoreconnaissance aircraft, delivered to the USAAF under the F-4 and F-5 designations. By April 1943 the Lockheed Model 422, the "ultimate Lightning," was ready for mass production. Equipped with Allison F-15 engines delivering 1,600 war-emergency horsepower, the Model 422s were durable and powerful fighters that earned the Lightning a deserved reputation as one of the best combat aircraft of World War II. The USAAF took delivery of 7,382 Lockheed Model 422s under the designations P-38H, P-38J, P-38K, and P-38L. The British Royal Air Force expressed an interest in the aircraft and ordered 243 under the designation Lightning I.

The Lightnings were mainly manufactured in Burbank, but the Vultee Aircraft Company also built 113 P-38Ls for the USAAF at their newly opened factory in Nashville, Tennessee. Lockheed built the photoreconnaissance Lightnings in Burbank, but installed the cameras at a modification center in Dallas.

Down the coast in San Diego, Consolidated was producing large numbers of its PBY Catalina flying boats and even larger numbers of its B-24 Liberator heavy bombers. Not to be overlooked in considering the

A dramatic nighttime view shows an early North American Mustang running up its Allison V1710 engine. *Library of Congress*

An early Allison-engined variant of the North American Mustang undergoes final assembly at Inglewood. *Courtesy Earl Blount*

production volume at Consolidated was the Downey, California, factory of Consolidated's soon-to-be sister company, the Vultee Aircraft Corporation. During the war, the busy Vultee factory built almost as many airframes—albeit small, single-engine aircraft—as Consolidated did at all of its factories combined.

As noted in the previous chapter, Consolidated's founder, Reuben Fleet, had sold his 34.26 percent controlling interest in Consolidated to Errett Lobban Cord's Avco (Vultee's parent firm) for $10.9 million just before Pearl Harbor. Avco then took steps toward merging Consolidated with Vultee, which it had controlled in various forms since the mid-1930s. The stock purchase was only the first step toward the merger of the two entities. In December 1941, the United States entered World War II and the necessity to gear up for wartime production took

precedence. The housekeeping details for the merger were worked out during 1942, and in March 1943 stockholders gave their final approval, creating Consolidated-Vultee Aircraft Corporation.

The name "Convair" as a contraction for Consolidated-Vultee Aircraft Corporation came about almost immediately, although it would not be an official corporate name until after World War II. The abbreviation was seen during the war as "ConVAir," "ConVair," and "Convair." The latter became standard by the end of the war, although Consolidated-Vultee remained the formal company name. (It is worth noting that the term "Consair" as an abbreviation for Consolidated Aircraft Company had also been in use before the merger. In 1954, the entity officially became the Convair Division of General Dynamics Corporation.)

continued on page 98

RIGHT: A production team at Inglewood, California, makes wiring assemblies at a junction box on the firewall for the right engine of a B-25 bomber. Forward of this wall, another crew will mount one of two Wright Cyclone engines. *Alfred Palmer, Office of War Information*

OPPOSITE: B-25 bombers are assembled at North American Aviation's inland expansion facility in Kansas City. *Alfred Palmer, Office of War Information*

Employees at North American Aviation in Inglewood assemble the cowling on Allison V1710s for the Mustang fighter planes. *Alfred Palmer, Office of War Information*

OPPOSITE: Metal parts are placed on Masonite before they slide under the multi-ton hydropress at North American Aviation. *Alfred Palmer, Office of War Information*

continued from page 95

As the merger was consummated, a new management team moved into place. Isaac "Mac" Laddon became general manager of Consolidated immediately upon Fleet's departure and was elected as a Vultee vice president as well. As chairman, Avco brought in Tom Girdler from their Republic Steel subsidiary and named Vultee chairman Harry Woodhead president.

When the United States entered World War II, Vultee was building trainers for the USAAF, including Vultee BT-13 Valiants at Downey and Stinson AT-19 Reliants in Wayne, Michigan. Other products included

the P-66 Vanguard fighter, ordered by Sweden but diverted to China, as well as the A-31 and A-35 Vengeance attack bombers for Britain's Royal Air Force. Reportedly, Lady Halifax, wife of Britain's ambassador to the United States, who visited Vultee during the summer of 1941, gave the Vengeance its name. During the war, production of these aircraft was centered mainly at the Vultee plant in Nashville, Tennessee.

Ultimately, the little Valiant would be one of the most successful aircraft in American aviation history, with 11,538 built before and during World War II. There was such a huge demand for trainers that sales of these small but ubiquitous craft helped propel Vultee and North

Early Mustang production in the days when the craft method was still alive and well on the floor at North American Aviation in Inglewood.
Courtesy Earl Blount

American Aviation into the top two slots among the companies within the American aircraft industry during World War II. At the end of 1943, it was reported that Vultee's Downey plant was working on the largest unit order ever placed by the War Department.

Consolidated would build 3,281 PBY Catalinas, mainly in San Diego, but the company's major project during World War II was the B-24 Liberator, which was produced in greater numbers than any other American warplane ever. According to company records, 18,482 Liberators were manufactured, including 6,726 built by Consolidated in San

Diego and 3,034 at a new facility the company operated in Fort Worth. Additional aircraft were produced under license by Douglas in Tulsa, Lockheed in Burbank, North American Aviation in Dallas, and the Ford Motor Company at a huge factory in Willow Run, Michigan, built specifically for the Liberator.

The XB-24 prototype made its debut flight in December 1939 and the first production series aircraft were ordered by France in June 1940 and the U.S. Army Air Corps in August of the same year. France was defeated by the Germans within days of placing their orders and the

LEFT: A North American Aviation technician at Inglewood prepares to install the spinner cap over a Mustang propeller. *Courtesy Earl Blount*

BELOW: B-25H Mitchells dominate this view of the ramp at North American Aviation, although there are some early-model Mustangs on the left and some AT-6 Texans in the background. *Boeing Archives*

export Liberators, designated LB-30, went to Britain. Early Air Corps orders were also diverted to Britain as the Liberator I, and the first B-24As reached the Air Corps as it became the USAAF in the summer of 1941.

The range and payload capacity also made the B-24 attractive as a transport for the new USAAF Ferrying Command (later the Air Transport Command). Transport versions included some that were converted from B-24s in the field, and some that came off the assembly line as transports. These included 284 C-87 Liberator Expresses and 209 C-109s that were built as B-24s but converted to haul fuel over the Himalayas to bases in China. The U.S. Navy also ordered a patrol bomber version of the B-24 that was designated PB4Y and known as the Privateer. The first 977 PB4Y-1 aircraft had the familiar twin verti-

cal tail surfaces of the B-24, while the later PB4Y-2, of which 736 were produced, had a single tall tailfin and rudder.

Across the nation, the American aircraft industry had mobilized with unimagined swiftness and proficiency. Reacting first in the summer of 1940, as France fell to the Germans, and with redoubled urgency after Pearl Harbor was attacked 18 months later, the industry would experience a tenfold increase in production.

In 1939, the first year of World War II, the American aircraft industry produced 2,141 military aircraft for the Army and Navy. This compared to 4,467 produced in Japan, 7,940 in the United Kingdom, and 8,295 in Germany. In 1940, the United States' output nearly tripled to 6,019, surpassing Japan's 4,768. In that year, the United

ABOVE: P-38 Lightnings crowd the Lockheed assembly line at Burbank, California. *Lockheed California Company*

OPPOSITE: A nearly completed P-38 Lightning is hoisted away from the assembly line at Burbank. *Lockheed California Company*

RIGHT: Dozens of P-38 Lightnings are parked outdoors on the ramp at Burbank for the final steps of production. Favorable weather gave California planemakers crucial additional factory space. *Lockheed California Company*

OPPOSITE: A technician at Vega Aircraft in Burbank, California, inspects electrical subassemblies probably destined for Ventura patrol aircraft. When the Office of War Information released this photo during World War II, it was accompanied by a caption that read in part, "Hollywood missed a good bet when they overlooked this attractive aircraft worker." Indeed, Hollywood was less than an hour's drive south of the factory where she worked. Perhaps she made her way to Tinseltown after the war. Her picture, but not her name, was in the files transferred to the Library of Congress when the OWI closed shop. *David Bransby, Office of War Information*

Kingdom's total also doubled to 15,049, while Germany increased only slightly to 10,826.

In was in 1941 that the American aircraft industry demonstrated a 323 percent growth rate, the greatest percentage increase in production in its history. The U.S. Army Air Corps, which became the autonomous USAAF on June 20 of that year, absorbed 45 percent of these aircraft. The remainder was divided between the U.S. Navy and export customers, primarily British Empire air forces, especially the United Kingdom and Canada. In the first quarter, the U.S. Army air arm took delivery of 1,105 aircraft, more than double its annual average for the 1930s. In the last quarter of the year—the same quarter that the United States entered World War II—the number increased to 3,417, but most of these aircraft were produced before December 7.

During 1942, as the American aircraft industry truly rolled up its sleeves to back the war effort, production levels nearly tripled again. From 19,433 aircraft in 1941, production rose 246 percent to 47,836—eight times the number produced just two years before in 1940. In 1941, 55 percent of the total, or 26,448 aircraft, went to the USAAF. The quarterly deliveries to the USAAF increased from 3,417 in the final quarter of 1941 to 7,842 in the final quarter of 1942.

All of this was made possible by the enormous increase in factory space. In 1940, the first year of industrial mobilization, $151 million

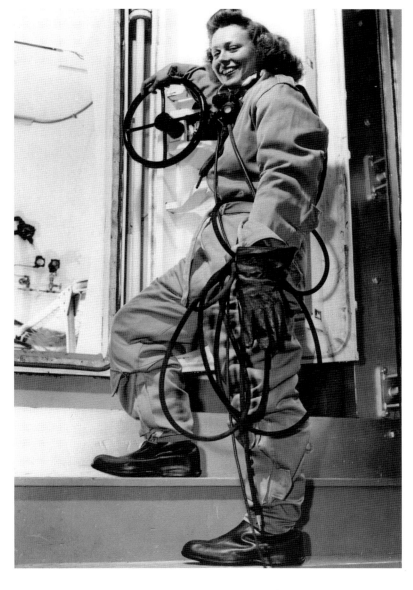

(approximately $2.1 billion in current dollars) was spent on plant expansion. In 1941, that number increased to $630 million (approximately $8.4 billion in current dollars), and in 1942, it more than doubled to $1.67 billion (approximately $20 billion in current dollars). About three-quarters of the dollar value investment in aircraft factory infrastructure to occur during World War II came in 1941 and 1942. The largest proportion of the nearly $3 billion that was spent by the United States government on facilities financing was the 61 percent that went into tooling, followed by 35 percent that went to the construction of buildings, and 4 percent spent on land purchases.

Thanks to the beginnings of industrial mobilization in 1940, most of American industry was on a war footing by January 1942. Most of

the American aircraft industry, in fact, was on a war footing within days—if not hours—of the news of the Pearl Harbor attack. Beginning in the spring of 1942, factories ran 24 hours a day and generally seven days a week.

As the industry geared up to address round-the-clock schedules and ballooning order books, work crews grew faster than at any time in the short history of the American aircraft industry. Men with technical skills were hired, as were men with only basic skills and an eagerness to learn. These new men were joined on the factory floor by a sizable number of women, because of the demand for men in the armed forces. In no major American industry was the proportion of women workers higher than it was in aviation. By 1944, 30 percent of working

ABOVE: Floyd Richlin consults with engineer Patsy Smith at her drafting table in the Consolidated plant in San Diego, circa 1943. Later, Smith suits up for a "flight" in the altitude chamber at Consolidated Vultee. *Author collection*

OPPOSITE: A group of sailors inspect a PV-1 Ventura being built for the U.S. Navy by Lockheed's Vega component in Burbank. *Lockheed California Company*

Mike Hazelip took this picture of PBY Catalinas on the Consolidated assembly line for release to the media. Before the censors would let it out, however, the identification numbers on the tails were painted out on the negative. *Author collection*

women had industrial jobs, triple the 1940 proportion. The total number of women in industrial jobs would peak at around 6 million. By 1945, one in every three workers was female, and the average income for women had risen by 38 percent.

The archetype of the woman war worker was "Rosie the Riveter," the character immortalized in the early 1943 hit song of the same name by Redd Evans and John Jacob Loeb. Rosie would get her visual dimension when Norman Rockwell painted her for the cover of the May 29, 1943, *Saturday Evening Post*.

The output of the American aircraft industry in 1942 dwarfed that of other leading powers. German production increased to 15,556 aircraft and United Kingdom production to 23,672, but United States numbers were better than both combined. In Japan, production increased, but only to 8,861 units. Soviet production for the year is said to have reached 25,436, but the American aircraft industry was as far ahead in quality as it was in quantity. The Red Air Force was keen to operate American equipment—in 1942 and 1943, 5 percent of the total American production was earmarked for lend-lease to the Soviets.

ABOVE: Seen here in April 1943, Wendell E. Smith had been the art director at Capper Publications for ten years when he joined Consolidated's Production Illustration Department in 1942. A self-styled "fireplace fanatic," he also contributed illustrations to *American Home* magazine under the pen name "Homer Hearthstone." *Author collection*

RIGHT: Drill press operators do handwork at Consolidated in San Diego. *Author collection*

A perfect job is revealed as the stencils are removed by this crew putting the United States insignia on a PBY Catalina at Consolidated. The time period is early 1942. In a few months, they will no longer be required to place the red "meatball" in the center, but by 1943, they'll have to paint bars on both sides of the star. *Author collection*

A technician at the Vultee plant in Nashville, Tennessee, pauses to smile for the photographer while working on a Vultee Vengeance dive bomber in February 1943. The USAAF operated Vengeances under the A-31 and A-35 designations. *Alfred Palmer, Office of War Information*

According to Irving Brinton Holley in the Center of Military History study *Buying Aircraft*, "Large or small, every manufacturer participating in the aircraft program was confronted with new and baffling problems imposed by the demands of war. Until these were resolved and output was accelerated, air arm leaders knew that air power would remain a concept rather than a reality."

By solving these myriad problems, both theoretical and practical, the American aircraft industry became the greatest planemaking entity that the world had seen, but even greater things were yet to come. As 1943 dawned, the American aircraft industry had not even begun to hit its stride.

LEFT: The tail surfaces of a Vultee Valiant are adjusted at the Downey, California, plant. According to USAAF records, during World War II, Vultee built 11,537 of these durable basic trainers for the USAAF at Downey under the BT-13 and BT-15 designations. *Author collection*

OPPOSITE: A worker at Vultee's Nashville plant makes final adjustments in the wheel well of an inner wing before the installation of the landing gear. This is one of the numerous assembly operations in the mass production of Vultee Vengeance dive bombers. *Alfred Palmer, Office of War Information*

Hoax Hamlets Fool the Enemy

An interesting and often overlooked footnote in the history of U.S. aircraft factories during World War II regards the novel steps that were taken to protect these production facilities from enemy air attack. This was especially true on the West Coast, where memories of the surprise air attack on Pearl Harbor haunted everyone. Many factories were within minutes of the ocean. Indeed, the Southern California factories were nearly all within one minute's flight time from the lapping waves of the Pacific.

Even before World War II, enemy air attack was considered such a threat that new aircraft factories supported by federal money were required to be well inland in states such as Missouri, Nebraska, Ohio, Oklahoma, and Tennessee.

Because of threat perceived in the wake of Pearl Harbor, the U.S. Army Corps of Engineers undertook to camouflage many of the West Coast plants. In Seattle, this included the entire Boeing Plant 2 complex.

In these camouflage projects, engineers got very creative, fabricating artificial cities atop the hangars in an effort to make the facilities appear to be innocuous residential neighborhoods when viewed from above. Fake houses were made of canvas and artificial trees were created with chicken wire matrices. "Streets" and "grass" were painted across runways. In Seattle, there was even a plan afoot to create a phony tributary for the Duwamish River in order to confuse enemy bombardiers. A major consultant to these projects was John Stewart Detlie, an architect and engineer who had worked as an art director at the Metro-Goldwyn-Mayer film Studio in Hollywood between 1935 and 1942.

By 1944, much of the camouflage was officially deemed unnecessary, but in many cases it was not fully removed until late in 1946

RIGHT: Two young Boeing employees stroll down Synthetic Street, about a block from its intersection with Burlap Boulevard. The people who staged the great rooftop camouflage projects certainly had a sense of humor. As the war came to a close and the camouflage was less important, companies staged photo-ops on the streets of their factory rooftop villages. *Boeing Archives*

OPPOSITE: The 26-acre "neighborhood" that engineers built atop Boeing's Plant 2 complex overlooked the Duwamish River. Known to Boeing employees as "Wonderland," it contained 53 homes, 24 garages, a gas station, a corner store, and three greenhouses. Until the final months of World War II, taking an aerial photo such as this was illegal. *Boeing Archives*

LEFT: Thanks to Hollywood set designers, this counterfeit neighborhood in Santa Monica looks pretty realistic, even at a low angle. It certainly would have kept bombardiers guessing. By 1945, when this picture was taken, the "streets" had developed a few "pot holes." *Courtesy Harry Gann*

RIGHT: It was the spring of 1945 and the threat of air attack on Southern California had faded, when Douglas staged this photo-op on the streets of its hoax hamlet in Santa Monica. Charlotte Reineke pretended to rake the artificial turf, while Louise Radcliffe hung out some laundry and Mickey Proctor scouted the area for a place to do some sunbathing. *Courtesy Harry Gann*

LEFT: Workers at the Douglas Aircraft Company plant in Santa Monica, California, go to work in 1944, ignoring the "faux forest" atop the plant. The trees were made of painted chicken feathers and wire. *Courtesy Harry Gann*

Chapter Four

The Peak of Production

B y 1943, thanks to the might of American industry—and the might of the American armed forces—the tide had finally begun to turn in World War II. After the defeat of the Imperial Japanese Navy—mainly by U.S. Navy air power—at the Battle of Midway in 1942, the Japanese were on the defensive. During 1943, the Allies pushed the Germans out of North Africa and Sicily, and fascist Italy had capitulated. Hitler's troops occupied Italy, but Allied troops—heavily supported by American-made warplanes—were pushing them back.

By the third quarter of 1943, the American aircraft factories had reached a level of production that could not have been imagined before the attack on Pearl Harbor a scant two years before. Deliveries to the USAAF in the last pre–Pearl Harbor quarter in 1941 were 2,383. Two years later, in the third quarter of 1943, the USAAF took delivery of 11,776 aircraft—five times as many—and that number would rise nearly 14 percent in the fourth quarter to 13,347. Further, the 45,889 aircraft received by the USAAF in 1943 represented just 53 percent of the total output of the American aircraft industry in 1943.

The January 19, 1942, issue of *Time* magazine waxed poetic when it expounded:

Let no man say it cannot be done. It must be done and we have undertaken to do it. Thus last week did the President launch the

biggest production program in world history. For 1942, United States industry is asked to produce 60,000 airplanes, 45,000 tanks, 20,000 anti-aircraft guns, 8,000,000 deadweight tons of merchant ships. For 1943, 125,000 planes, 75,000 tanks, 35,000 anti-aircraft guns, 10,000,000 tons of merchant ships. Even in billion-calloused, production-booming January 1942, these figures at first seemed fantastic. Only 18 months ago, United States output was around 500 planes monthly.

In fact, the American aircraft industry would produce 47,836 aircraft in 1942 and 85,898 in 1943. Though less than the dreams of early 1942, this was more aircraft than were produced by any country in any year in history, before or since—except for the American aircraft industry itself in 1944.

RIGHT: Virginia Davis, a riveter in the Assembly and Repair Department of the Corpus Christi Naval Air Base, supervises Charles Potter, a trainee from Michigan. The Office of War Information caption that accompanied this photo during the war reads, "After eight weeks of training he will go into civil service. Should he be inducted or enlist in the armed service, he will be valuable to mechanized units of the Army or Navy." *Howard Hollem, Office of War Information*

OPPOSITE: Irma Lee McElroy, a former office worker, paints the American insignia on airplane wings at the Naval Air Base in Corpus Christi, Texas. When the Office of War Information released this photo during the war, the caption noted that she did her work "with precision and patriotic zeal." Her husband was a flight instructor at the base. *Howard Hollem, Office of War Information*

In 1943, German production rose to 25,527, and United Kingdom production to 26,263. Japanese production in 1943 had doubled to 16,693, but even the aggregate of all three was less than that of the United States. Soviet production, including that of the new factories east of the Ural Mountains, exceeded 34,000 in 1943—still less than half of what was produced by the American aircraft industry.

According to Alan Milward, writing in *War, Economy, and Society*, "Despite the almost-continual crises of the civilian war agencies, the American economy expanded at an unprecedented (and unduplicated) rate between 1941 and 1945. The gross national product of the United States, as measured in constant dollars, grew from $88.6 billion in 1939—while the country was still suffering from the depression—to $135 billion in 1944. War-related production skyrocketed from just 2 percent of GNP to 40 percent in 1943."

Often overlooked in the story of American aircraft production during World War II is the work that was done in terms of upgrades and modifications. During the war, and since, it has been a characteristic of military aircraft development that the design is never static. Throughout this book, we have seen initial production types of a particular aircraft given an "A" suffix, an improved variant arriving on the scene with a "B" suffix, and so on. In Chapter 2, we saw how constant evolution frustrated efforts by the American automobile industry to

Under the close supervision of the foreman, a new Wright R2600 Cyclone engine assembly is installed in a B-25 bomber at North American's Inglewood, California, plant. *Alfred Palmer, Office of War Information*

adapt mass production techniques to aircraft manufacturing. For the American aircraft industry, when the quantities were relatively small and production was more leisurely, aircraft were "shop engineered" on the assembly line and model changes were relatively easy.

As World War II intensified, however, with monthly output mushrooming and change orders coming in constantly, the almost haphazard method of shop-engineered model changes became problematic. The U.S. Army Air Forces' logistics and maintenance system began to lose track of exactly what equipment was built into which model. Upgrades to radios, carburetors, or landing-gear struts might be made within a model series without a change in designation, which became perplexing for crews using and maintaining aircraft in the field.

A form of standardization was necessary, and the American aircraft industry was compelled to borrow a page from its cousins in the American automobile industry: the scheduled model change. For years, automakers had an annual model change inserted into their production schedules at a known, fixed point. Planemakers had never done this. Because of the urgencies of wartime scheduling and rapid technological changes, an annual model change was out of the question, so the Production Division of the USAAF Materiel Command at Wright Field introduced the Block System.

Under the Block System, a production series was broken into numbered groupings called blocks. Major variant changes were still given suffix letter changes, but within these variants, there were multiple

Employees at work on the "Sunshine Assembly Line" in Inglewood, near today's Los Angeles International Airport, trim out North American B-25 Mitchell bombers. Because of the good weather in Southern California, final assembly could be done outdoors. *Alfred Palmer, Office of War Information*

LEFT: P-51D Mustangs on the North American Aviation assembly line. The Mustang established itself as the best Allied fighter to see combat in World War II. *Courtesy Earl Blount*

OPPOSITE: Part of the cowling for one of the Wright R2600 Cyclones for a B-25 bomber is assembled in the Engine Department of North American's Inglewood factory. *Alfred Palmer, Office of War Information*

predetermined blocks. Any changes were scheduled to coincide with a scheduled block change.

Take, for example, the Lockheed P-38 Lightning. There were five production blocks of the P-38F, averaging about 105 aircraft per block, and there were six production blocks for the subsequent P-38G variant. The latter blocks ranged in size from a dozen units to 548 units, and averaged 180. The changeover from the P-38F to the P-38G required 23,250 engineering hours and 23,760 tooling hours. The change from the P-38G-3 block to the P-38G-5 block took an estimated 5,000 engineering hours and 4,000 tooling hours.

In some cases, there were just a few blocks within a variant, and in other cases, many. The Boeing B-17F production series contained 56 production blocks, while the B-17G series comprised 48. To the casual observer, the two variants are identical except for the changes in nose armament and the addition of the "chin" turret on the B-17G. Most changes were in the form of nuances known only to those flying or maintaining the equipment.

Another aspect of the constant evolution of American warplanes was the many changes and modifications not made at factories. These occurred at field locations that ranged from overseas bases to about

The importance of eye protection when drilling metal is demonstrated by these two workers assembling a wing section for a North American P-51 Mustang fighter aircraft. Soon, this airplane would be escorting Eighth Air Force heavy bombers taking the war to the heart of Hitler's Third Reich. *Alfred Palmer, Office of War Information*

two dozen depots and modification centers in the United States. Officially, the USAAF estimated that by 1944 a quarter of all modification work was done away from the factories, including at depots operated by the services themselves, especially the U.S. Navy facility at Corpus Christi, Texas.

Gradually, much of the modification work was concentrated at two large facilities: the Bechtel-McCone-Parson center in Birmingham, Alabama, and the United Air Lines maintenance center in Cheyenne, Wyoming. In fact, when an improved tail turret was designed for later-block B-17Gs, nearly all of the so-called "Cheyenne Turrets" were installed by United rather than by the manufacturers.

In the United States, the aircraft industry was also achieving economies of scale by 1944. According to the *USAAF Statistical Digest*, before the war, the unit cost of a Consolidated B-24 had gone from $379,162 to $215,516. Lockheed billed the government $134,280 for a P-38 before the war and $97,147 for a much more capable variant of the same aircraft in 1944. Douglas charged $128,761 for a C-47 before and $88,574 in 1944. In 1941, a Boeing B-17 cost $301,221, while in

1944 it was down to $204,370. Production had become more efficient, as well. In 1941, 55,000 man hours were needed to turn out a B-17. By 1944, this had dropped to 19,000 hours. Of course, by 1944, the hours were no longer "man" hours, because nearly half—and in some cases more than half—of the workforce were women.

An accomplishment of perhaps equal importance to the great volume of production achieved by the American aircraft industry was its capability for incredibly swift technological innovation. A case in point is that of the North American Aviation P-51 Mustang, generally recognized

as the most exceptional USAAF fighter of World War II. That in itself makes the Mustang special, but what truly sets it apart is that it was developed entirely during the war and it arrived in time to make a difference in tactical operations. Most of the war's remarkable aircraft were already on the drawing boards when World War II began in September 1939, and early variants of many were already flying. In the case of the Mustang, however, the very idea of it occurred after that date.

Late in 1939, Britain's Royal Air Force needed more and more fighter aircraft, but the British aircraft manufacturing capacity was

A painter prepares the natural metal surface on the tail of a North American P-51 Mustang for paint. Soon the reflection of the bright Southern California sun will be dulled by olive-drab paint. *Alfred Palmer, Office of War Information*

P-51D Mustangs undergo final assembly outdoors at the North American Aviation factory in Inglewood. These men are working on the fighter's six wing-mounted Browning .50-caliber machine guns. The camouflage tarp above afforded some protection from the bright California sun. *Courtesy Earl Blount*

pushed to the limit. To supplement British production, the Royal Air Force was getting all the P-40-type fighters they could from Curtiss, but they needed even more. With this in mind, the British Air Ministry came to the United States looking for a second production line for the P-40. The British delegation asked North American Aviation whether they could build P-40 types. The answer was in the affirmative, and North American purchased P-40 blueprints. In the meantime, however, John Leland "Lee" Atwood, North American's chief engineer, had developed what he proposed was a better idea. He said that his team could create a fighter using the same Allison V1710 inline engine found in the P-40s but superior to the Curtiss aircraft. After extensive and ongoing discussions, he convinced Sir Henry Self, the head of the British delegation, and the project got under way.

The North American Model NA-73X, nicknamed Mustang, was designed and built in 117 days and first flew in October 1940. The U.S. Army Air Corps (USAAF after June 1941) took a passing interest in the sleek new plane and ordered two for tests under the designation XP-51 and the given name Apache. The first of 620 Mustang I production air-

North American Aviation technician Gerry Williams poses cheerfully with a 75mm shell beneath the muzzle of the nose-mounted cannon in this B-25 Mitchell. *Courtesy Earl Blount*

The fuselage of a P-51D Mustang is mated with the wing assembly. During 1944 and 1945, scenes similar to this were repeated more than 6,500 times in Inglewood, California, and nearly 1,500 times in Dallas, Texas. *Courtesy Earl Blount*

craft reached the Royal Air Force in April 1941 and tests showed them to outperform the P-40. They even topped the great Supermarine Spitfire in low-altitude operations.

Ironically, the next USAAF production order for the airplane destined to become the best USAAF fighter of World War II cast it as a dive bomber. Produced as N-97, it was basically an NA-73X fitted with dive brakes. Designated as A-36A and called the Invader, 500 NA-97 dive bombers were delivered to the USAAF, with which they would see service in Sicily and Italy in 1943.

The A-36As were followed by the P-51A series intended for delivery to the USAAF and immediate transferal to the RAF as Mustang IIs.

Most, however, were retained by the USAAF and assigned to the Fourteenth Air Force in the China-Burma-India Theater, where they turned in a remarkably good performance against Japanese air and ground forces during 1943.

The Allison V-1710 engine that was standard equipment in the thousand RAF Mustangs and USAAF P-51s and 500 A-36As prior to the end of 1942 had made it a surprisingly reliable and capable airplane—but not a great airplane. In the spring of 1942, however, the RAF had experimented with the idea of retrofitting Mustangs with the Rolls-Royce Merlin 61 engine. The resulting aircraft, unofficially called the Mustang X, was amazingly powerful and reviewers were unanimous in their praise.

The case of the Merlin engine is significant. The story of Anglo-American relations with regard to World War II aircraft production often seems like a one-way street. Almost one in four aircraft bought by the British during World War II were American-made, while the American armed forces used negligible numbers of British aircraft. With the Merlin engine, the transatlantic flow was east to west. More Merlin engines were built in the United States than any other inline water-cooled aircraft engine, except for the Allison V1710, and most of the latter were built relatively early in the war.

With a licensing arrangement from Rolls-Royce, Packard built 54,714 Merlins in Detroit, and Continental built 797 in Muskegon,

Michigan. With these, North American was able to plan a series of factory-built Merlin-powered Mustangs. Designated as P-51Bs, these Mustangs started reaching the USAAF in May 1943. The long-range escort capability of the Mustang was the key reason that it is regarded as one of World War II's most important fighters, but this capability was not realized until the P-51B entered service.

The definitive Mustang was the P-51D. Earlier Mustangs were hindered by the lack of rearward visibility, but North American solved the problem with a full bubble canopy that afforded the pilot a 360-degree field of vision. The new Mustang went into full-scale *continued on page 135*

The North American Aviation flight line at Inglewood as it appeared in 1945. In the foreground are Mustangs destined for both the USAAF and Britain's Royal Air Force, and in the background are several AT-6 Texan advanced trainers. By this time, production of trainers had tapered off considerably from the frantic days of 1942. *Author collection*

With a load of wing sections on his flatbed, Douglas truck driver Ralph Tikker picks up his delivery paperwork from dispatcher Earl Doran in June 1943. *Courtesy Harry Gann*

Young employees in the Douglas Aircraft Company Armaments Department seem pleased with this brace of Browning heavy machine guns destined for Douglas warplanes.
Courtesy Harry Gann

Young newcomers to the gunsmith's trade get some pointers from an old hand at the Douglas Aircraft Company Armaments Department. *Courtesy Harry Gann*

FAR LEFT: Making an adjustment to a Browning .50-caliber machine gun at the Douglas Aircraft Company Armaments Department. *Courtesy Harry Gann*

LEFT: A drill bit is changed during some work in the tight spaces of what appears to be an aircraft tail section. *Author collection*

continued from page 131
production at the Inglewood, California, factory in February 1944 and at Dallas in July.

According to company records North American Aviation produced 15,575 Mustangs, including 7,956 P-51Ds. Of the "D" variant, 82 percent were built in Inglewood, the remainder in Dallas. Previously, 1,988 P-51Bs were built in Inglewood, and 1,750 similar P-51Cs were built in Dallas. From just 57 Mustangs at the end of 1942, USAAF inventory increased to 1,165 at the end of 1943, to 3,914 at the end of 1944, and to 5,595 at the end of June 1945.

As with North American Aviation and its Mustang, Douglas also developed an aircraft entirely during the war that can be included among the technological and tactical best of the war. The A-26

Invader attack bomber, like the Mustang fighter, also had a career after World War II. In fact, the type (redesignated the B-26 after 1948) was still in service in the Vietnam War, although production had long since ceased. The A-26 program stood technologically on the shoulders of Douglas' earlier and very successful Boston/Havoc program. The Invader was essentially a faster and more capable aircraft in the same size and weight class. The XA-26 prototype made its first flight on July 10, 1942, and production models were in service a year later. The first production series was the solid-nose A-26B, of which 1,174 were built at Long Beach, while 205 were built at the new Douglas factory in Tulsa, Oklahoma.

Five A-26C-DLs were completed at Long Beach before all Invader production shifted to Tulsa. The Oklahoma plant was to have built

A riveting machine operator at the Douglas Aircraft Company's Long Beach, California, plant joins sections of wing ribs to reinforce the inner wing assemblies of B-17F Flying Fortress heavy bombers. *Alfred Palmer, Office of War Information*

3,895 A-26C-DTs, but only 1,086 were completed before production was terminated by the end of World War II.

Another important wartime program for Douglas was not a warplane, but an aircraft that was originally supposed to have represented a new milestone for the company in the field of commercial air travel. The Douglas DC-4 would be the first commercially successful, American four-engine landplane propliner. While its commercial success would not come until after World War II, it was conceived and first flown before the war and the first production series DC-4s were on the assembly line in Santa Monica in December 1941 when the Japanese bombed Pearl Harbor.

Donald Douglas had started development of his four-engine DC-4 even before his remarkable DC-3 made its maiden flight in 1935. It was to be capable of carrying more than twice as many passengers as its ubiquitous predecessor. The first 24 of 61 DC-4s that were on order were nearing completion when the United States entered World War II. Recognizing the value of the DC-4 as a military transport, the USAAF commandeered the 24 aircraft already on the assembly line, putting them into service as military transports under the designation C-54. The USAAF then took over existing orders and increased them to 252 that would be built to military specs as the C-54A. During 1942 and 1943, the USAAF placed a series of orders for C-54B aircraft similar to the C-54As,

An inspector confers with a worker as she makes a careful check of center wings for C-47 transport planes at the Douglas Long Beach plant. *Alfred Palmer, Office of War Information*

but with provisions for stretcher racks for evacuating severely wounded personnel from the war zones to hospitals in the United States. To supplement production, Douglas opened a new facility near Chicago that eventually evolved into today's O'Hare International Airport.

Douglas built 100 C-54B-DOs in Santa Monica and 120 C-54B-DCs in Chicago, and thereafter all production was shifted to the latter facility. This included 380 C-54D-DCs and 125 C-54E-DCs. Between 1942 and 1945, the USAAF C-54 fleet averaged more than 20 flights a day across the rugged North Atlantic. By the end of the war in Europe, these Sky-masters, as they came to be known, successfully completed 79,642 transoceanic flights with only three ditchings, one of which was a test.

The C-54 was also one of the aircraft to benefit most from mass production in terms of its unit cost. When the DC-4s were commandeered off the assembly line after Pearl Harbor, they were among the most expensive aircraft in the USAAF, at $516,552 apiece. By 1943, with the development costs better amortized, the unit cost was down to $400,831, and in 1944 it cost the USAAF just $285,113 to buy a Skymaster.

Down the coast at Hawthorne, the most illustrious of Douglas alumni was also doing some technologically groundbreaking work. A designer with an excellent reputation for his work at Lockheed and Douglas, Jack Northrop had started and operated two small manufac-turing firms of his own in the 1920s and 1930s. He left the second, in

which Don Douglas owned a 51 percent share, in 1939 to start his third, Northrop Aircraft. He set up shop in Hawthorne, where he would build the remarkable Northrop P-61 Black Widow radar-equipped night fighter. Beginning in October 1943, Jack Northrop delivered 200 production model P-61As, followed by 450 improved P-61Bs beginning in August 1944. The more powerful P-61D debuted in July 1944, but only 41 of the 517 on order were completed before World War II ended. During the last year of World War II, the P-61 earned a reputation as an extraordinary night fighter, certainly the best such aircraft purposely built for that role by the American aircraft industry.

At Lockheed in Burbank, the major products at the peak of wartime production were very large numbers of P-38s, while Lockheed's Vega subsidiary built B-17s for the USAAF, and PV-1 Ventura and PV-2 Harpoon patrol planes for the U.S. Navy and the Royal Air Force.

One of the great production stories to come out of the annals of the American aircraft industry during World War II was that of multi-site, multi-manufacturer production pooling to construct USAAF heavy bombers. While the Boeing-designed B-17 Flying Fortress was produced not only in Seattle by Boeing, but also in Southern California by Douglas and by Lockheed's Vega subsidiary under the Boeing-Douglas-Vega (BDV) Committee arrangement, this story pales in complexity when compared to that of the Consolidated B-24 Liberator.

As mentioned in Chapter 3, 18,482 Liberators were manufactured by five factories in four states. These factories (and their designation suffixes) included Consolidated's flagship factory in San Diego (CO), as well as sites in Dallas (NT), Fort Worth (CF), Tulsa (DT), and Willow Run, Michigan (FO). The initial work was done at the Consolidated flagship factory complex in San Diego in the three years prior to the United States' entry into World War II. By December 1941, initial production models had been delivered to both the U.S. Army Air Forces and Britain's Royal Air Force. In January 1942, Consolidated rolled out the first B-24D, the variant earmarked to test mass production of very large aircraft on a scale that had never been seen.

Most of the B-24Ds, a total of 2,415, would be built in San Diego as B-24D-COs, but by late spring, the first of the satellite factories was on line and rolling out Liberators. Ground was broken in May 1941 for the factory on 563 acres on the north side of Fort Worth. With its visually spectacular mile-long assembly line, the government-owned factory was officially designated as Air Force Plant 4 but known locally as "the bomber plant." It was on the west side of the runway of the USAAF facility known as Tarrant Field until 1943, as Fort Worth Army Air Field until January 1948, and later as Carswell Air Force Base.

The mover and shaker behind locating Plant 4 at Fort Worth was the newspaperman and entrepreneur Amon Carter, a tireless civic booster for the city. When the United States government got into the business of aiding the expansion of the American aircraft industry through the Defense Plant Corporation and other agencies, the paradigm

LEFT: Sporting a brand-new pair of work gloves (possibly acquired expressly for the photo session), this young worker not only built airplanes, the wings she wears suggest that she also *flew* them. Alternatively, the wings might belong to a special friend who was in the service. *Courtesy Harry Gann*

OPPOSITE: The iron used here to solder an electrical connection appears cumbersome by today's standards. *Courtesy Harry Gann*

During World War II, the USAAF reckons that Douglas Aircraft Company built 1,155 A-26 Invader attack bombers in Long Beach and another 1,291 in Tulsa, Oklahoma. *Courtesy Harry Gann*

was to locate the new factories inland. With this in mind, Carter led a Fort Worth Chamber of Commerce public relations drive aimed at luring aircraft manufacturers. As early as 1939, Carter had been on the phone with Dutch Kindelberger at North American Aviation and Reuben Fleet at Consolidated, extolling tax incentives, a large labor pool, and the area's location as a rail and highway hub.

Fort Worth was not alone. Their neighboring rival city, Dallas, also hoped to lure California planemakers to a site on Mountain Creek west of the Hensley Reserve Airfield. Dallas, of course, could offer the same

incentives in terms of transportation and labor pool. After both showed some interest in the Dallas site, North American Aviation located there and Consolidated moved into the location near Fort Worth championed by Carter. In the meantime, Carter had also convinced the USAAF to install a major flight-training operation at Tarrant Field.

The Consolidated factory was completed in less than nine months and the first B-24 rolled off the assembly line in April 1942, 364 days after the groundbreaking. Through the next three years, employment at the facility mushroomed to nearly 40,000. Many of those workers were

War workers stream out the doors of the Lockheed plant in Burbank during a shift change in 1943. *Lockheed California Company*

ABOVE: Lockheed quality inspector Claire Nichols checks the canopy on a P-38 Lightning at Burbank, circa 1943. *Lockheed California Company*

ABOVE RIGHT: Sisters Jean and Joan Wickmire worked as a team at the Lockheed Burbank factory during World War II. *Lockheed California Company*

women who previously never would have had the opportunity for industrial jobs. The plant was also a boon to small nearby towns such as Cleburne, Decatur, and Denton. Meanwhile, a new neighborhood called Liberator Village formed around the south gate of the bomber plant and became home to thousands of aircraft workers who moved in from outside the area.

A third of all B-24s would be built at the huge factory constructed by the Ford Motor Company at Willow Run, near Detroit. Official U.S. Army records list 6,792 Liberators having been built here, compared to 6,729 in San Diego and 2,743 in Fort Worth. During 1944 alone, it is reckoned that 92 million pounds of airframe weight rolled out of Willow Run, more than half of what was produced in all German factories that year.

The facility at Willow Run was one of the largest industrial plants in the world and certainly among the most modern. It comprised 16 buildings on 67 acres, with two vast production bays that were 1.2 miles long, 150 feet wide, and 30 feet high. A small army of industrial cranes with a 38,000-pound capacity ran on overhead rails. These cranes could lift an entire unfueled Liberator with a couple of tons to spare.

The story of Willow Run dates back to 1940, when President Roosevelt's production boss, William S. Knudsen, had toyed with the notion of putting the immense capacity and expertise of the automobile industry to work building military aircraft. For reasons detailed in Chapter 2, such a wholesale conversion of factory operations did not occur, but there were exceptions.

A technician on the flight line at Burbank adjusts a fuselage panel on a P-38 Lightning. *Lockheed California Company*

ABOVE: William H. Moody, a wartime tool designer with Consolidated-Vultee, began his aviation career helping the Wright brothers design their first monoplane. *Author collection*

ABOVE RIGHT: It was raining during the April 18, 1941, groundbreaking for the Consolidated-Vultee plant in Fort Worth, Texas, but it didn't dampen the spirits of General Gerald Brant or Fort Worth city father Amon Carter. It was Carter's tireless promotional efforts that brought the plant to Fort Worth. It was still operating in the twenty-first century. *Author collection*

Many automobile companies were used to build parts and sub-assemblies, and most were content with such a role. Not so the Ford Motor Company. In the summer of 1941, Ford received a major sub-assembly contract for the B-24 program. However, Ford executives were very keen to see their role change from a parts supplier to a plane-maker. Indeed, Ford was quick to invest its own money to design and build expensive tooling and to create an infrastructure capable of man-ufacturing entire airplanes. Ford was sure it had the expertise to do this, and in October 1941 the USAAF was finally convinced to issue a contract to Ford for complete aircraft.

Early in 1941, the automaker had sent a team of about 200 to San Diego to go through Consolidated's files and copy 30,000 drawings and blueprints. At this point, there was an interesting—and for Ford, a frustrating—clash of cultures. First, the Ford people discovered that the Consolidated documents were written in a language other than that used in comparable automobile industry documents. It was then standard within the American aircraft industry to record measure-ments in fractions, while in Detroit, measurements were in decimals. A part that measured 10⅜ x 11½ x 32¾ in San Diego was 10.6 x 11.5 x 32.75 in Detroit. All 30,000 Consolidated drawings and blueprints had to be translated and redrawn.

Furthermore, aircraft engineers knew that their drawings would be read by experienced foremen and workers. In the automobile industry, almost nobody had experience in building machines as complex as air-craft. Things that could be taken for granted in San Diego had to be explicitly spelled out in Detroit.

It was not until April 1942 that Ford had one complete set of tool-ing in place at Willow Run. As Irving Brinton Holley points out in his Center of Military History study, *Buying Aircraft*:

The Ford engineers had planned to use dies far more extensively than was customary among the old-line aircraft firms. By using dies for

Wing sections for B-24 Liberators are built at Consolidated-Vultee. The engines were installed before the wings were mated with the fuselage. *Author collection*

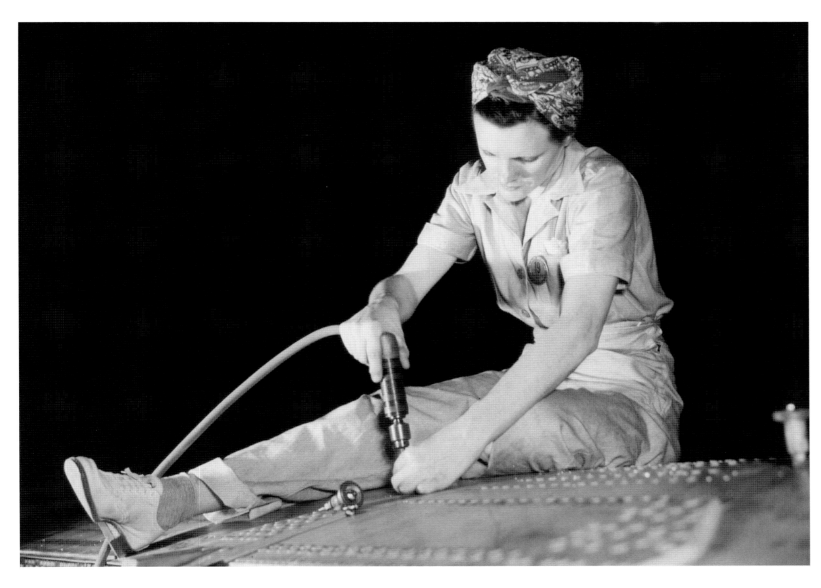

LEFT: A technician poses with a hand drill in a fuselage section of a Vultee Vengeance dive bomber at the company's facility in Nashville, Tennessee. Had she actually been working, rather than merely striking a pose for Alfred Palmer, she would have selected a much shorter drill bit. *Alfred Palmer, Office of War Information*

OPPOSITE: Grace Janota had been a shop clerk when she joined Consolidated-Vultee as a lathe operator at the Fort Worth plant. *Howard Hollem, Office of War Information*

blanking, piercing, forming, and drawing, the production men hoped to reach hitherto undreamed of levels of output. Once set up, tested, gauged, and put into action, high-speed presses manned by relatively unskilled employees could turn out extremely accurate parts in large quantities in very little time. Dies were expensive and hard to make. They required the services of highly skilled die-sinkers and the use of special machine tools. But in these resources the Ford empire was rich. The Ford toolmakers were world famous and the Ford tool room no less so. For example, in the main tool room the B-24 engineers had, in addition to the usual array of standard machine tools, a battery of 23 hard-to-get Kellett profilers, each worth $80,000, ready to cut the dies needed for the bomber program. Here were resources far beyond those possessed by any of the aircraft manufacturers.

However, as Holley continued:

The Ford plan to make maximum use of dies proved disappointing. To begin with, the production men had to learn from bitter experience that aluminum is not the same thing as steel. When they began using their forming dies on aluminum sheets, they discovered that the dies scratched and defaced the surface of the stock, which was considerably softer than steel. Scarred surfaces cannot be tolerated on aircraft exteriors for aerodynamic reasons, so it was absolutely essential to correct this difficulty. A trial of chrome plated die proved abortive. After considerable experimentation, it turned out that highly polished steel dies would work acceptably. But all this took time, the very item the production engineers had hoped to save by the use of dies.

147

This photograph affords a view of the mating operation on a C-87 transport plane just before it went to the pre-assembly line at the Consolidated-Vultee plant in Fort Worth, Texas. The C-87 was the transport version of the B-24 bomber. The USAAF officially noted that 291 of such aircraft were built at Fort Worth. *Howard Hollem, Office of War Information*

Holley went on to explain that Ford's whole program rested on the premise that the production techniques of the automobile industry could be applied directly to aircraft. Experience showed this was not quite true, and Ford spent more than $75 million (approximately $843 million in current dollars) on tooling alone. However, when the Willow Run plant was finally up and running, it was arguably the most efficient airplane factory in the world. For example, when the plant was running at full tilt, there were seven banks of wing-assembly fixtures, each holding five wings, so that 35 wing assemblies could be manufactured simultaneously. Built by Ingersoll, the massive wing-center section jig provided perfect accuracy, and completed 42 machining operations in

3 1/2 man hours, when, according to Holley, such a task required 500 man hours with regular tooling.

The money invested in machine tools of such precision was vital because the labor force was essentially inexperienced in making airplanes. At its apogee in 1944, Willow Run employed 42,500 people, of whom only 10,000 were Ford employees from other units with mass production experience.

One of the drawbacks of the highly automated system was that when design changes came along they were easier to incorporate into a shop-engineered aircraft than one on an assembly line. At Willow Run, when a model change came, the whole assembly line had to be shut

Crews at the end of the Consolidated Aircraft Corporation's mile-long assembly line in Fort Worth, Texas, ready a nose door for installation in a C-87 transport aircraft. *Howard Hollem, Office of War Information*

down for retooling. Under the Block System, however, the stoppages could be minimized and efficiency maintained. Nevertheless, the complexity of the Liberator meant that there were numerous master changes. One of the largest transformations came on March 15, 1943, when 95 master changes were made in the changeover from the B-24E-FO-5 to the B-24E-FO-10. Just 12 days and 57 aircraft later, 27 further master changes separated the B-24E-FO-10 from the B-24E-FO-15.

In man-hour terms, it took Willow Run 18 minutes to complete each pound of airframe weight, compared to an industry average of 28 minutes. That was good, but not as impressive as it might have been had it not taken three years for Willow Run to reach peak efficiency, and

had the USAAF need for heavy bombers not finally reached a plateau during the first half of 1944.

In March 1944, Willow Run achieved a monthly output of 309 finished aircraft—*10 per day*—plus complete sets of parts for another 112 (a calculated total of 421 Liberators). Ford estimated the maximum capacity of Willow Run to be 600 aircraft per month, but this was never realized because by this time, the USAAF could not absorb Liberators at that rate. At their peak inventory in 1944, the USAAF had 6,043 B-24s in service, including 3,808 operational with combat units overseas.

The first Liberator variants to be mass-produced in large numbers were the B-24D and the generally similar B-24E. Most of the former

The finishing touches are put on the 5,000th B-24 Liberator (tail number 44-41064), built during World War II. Boeing named its 5,000th B-17 *5 Grand*, and Consolidated-Vultee named its 5,000th Liberator *V Grand*. The double entendre, of course, was that "V" stood both for "5" and for "Victory." This San Diego–built Block 195 B-24J went on to serve with the USAAF Fifteenth Air Force in the Mediterranean Theater. *Author collection*

An unprecedented effort made the B-24 the most widely produced American warplane ever. Consolidated-Vultee records list 18,482 Liberators having been built, including 6,726 by the company in San Diego and 3,034 at a new facility that the company operated in Fort Worth. Additional aircraft were produced under license by Douglas in Tulsa, Lockheed in Burbank, and North American Aviation in Dallas. The greatest number, 6,792 were made by the Ford Motor Company at a huge factory in Willow Run, Michigan, built specifically for the Liberator. *Author collection*

A Pratt & Whitney R1830 Twin Wasp engine is installed in a B-24E Liberator at the Ford Motor Company factory in Willow Run, Michigan. *Howard Hollem, Office of War Information*

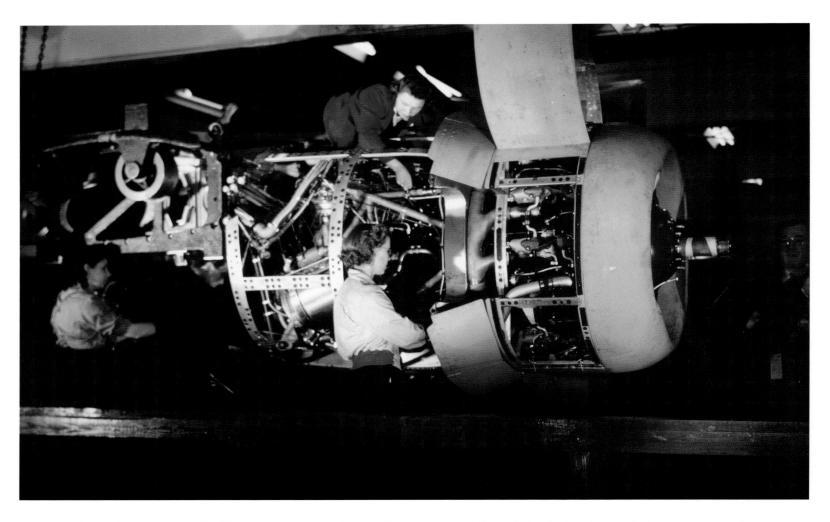

were manufactured in San Diego; all of the latter were not. As large-scale production of Liberators got underway at plants other than San Diego, it initially involved the final assembly of the aircraft using subassemblies that had been produced in San Diego. Gradually the manufacture of the subassemblies themselves was phased in at satellite sites. Consolidated built 2,415 B-24D-COs in San Diego and completed 303 B-24D-CFs in Fort Worth. The latter factory rolled out 144 B-24E-CFs at the latter site, while Douglas built 10 B-24D-DTs and 167 B-24E-DTs at Tulsa.

The next large mass production run of Liberators included the B-24H, built entirely at satellite locations, and the similar B-24J series, built mainly at the Consolidated factories in San Diego and Fort Worth. These aircraft boasted more powerful engines than earlier variants, plus more defensive armament in the form of a retractable, powered Sperry ball turret and a powered Emerson turret in the nose. Ford built 1,780 B-24H-FOs at Willow Run, 738 B-24H-CFs were built at Fort Worth, and Douglas produced 582 B-24H-DTs in Tulsa. San Diego rolled out 2,792 B-24J-COs, Fort Worth built 1,558 B-24J-CFs, Douglas built 205

B-24J-DTs, and North American Aviation manufactured 536 B-14J-NTs at Dallas. The final mass production of Liberators included the B-24L and B-24M series, both of which were built mainly at San Diego and at Willow Run. The totals included 417 B-24L-COs, 1,250 B-24L-FOs, 916 B-24M-COs, and 1,677 B-24M-FOs.

In the Pacific Northwest, the principal product at Boeing continued to be the remarkable B-17. Though Douglas and Lockheed built Flying Fortresses in Southern California as well, Boeing built the lion's share at its Plant 2 at Boeing Field, just south of downtown Seattle. During World War II, the company was under the management of Clairmont L. "Claire" Egtvedt and Philip G. "Phil" Johnson. Both men had been hired by Bill Boeing personally during the previous world war when they were just promising young engineering grads from the University of Washington.

Egtvedt became president in 1933 and acting chairman in 1934 when both Bill Boeing and Phil Johnson left in the wake of the collapse of the United Aircraft & Transport Corporation (UATC) holding company and the withdrawal of airmail contracts from private industry. The latter were eventually restored, but Bill Boeing stayed in retirement. Phil Johnson returned as president of Boeing in 1939 and Egtvedt was officially named as chairman. During the war, as in the 1930s, the top management at Boeing was well served by such imaginative and forward-thinking engineering talent as senior vice presidents Wellwood Beall and Edward Curtis Wells.

The pressure-cooker environment of the war years took its toll on Johnson, however. On September 14, 1944, while visiting the Boeing Wichita plant, he suffered a stroke and died. After Johnson's death, Egtvedt served again as both president and chairman until William McPherson "Bill" Allen became president in 1945.

As North American had engineered its Mustang entirely during the war, Boeing, too, developed during the war a remarkable aircraft that played a decisive role in the outcome. At the time considered one of the most extraordinary warplanes in the world—a true secret weapon—the Boeing B-29 Superfortress embodied all the principles of long-range strategic air power that had been theorized before the war and proven during the war by aircraft such as Boeing's own B-17. The Superfortress was the largest bomber to go into production during World War II and it had the longest range.

Four months after the start of World War II in Europe, the U.S. Army Air Corps solicited top-secret design proposals from aircraft builders for a bomber with a range of 5,333 miles and that could carry a full bomb load 2,000 miles from its base. Boeing had been studying such an aircraft since the mid-1930s and put together a team of designers that included Ed Wells, the engineer who had proved himself so well in the design of the B-17. The company submitted a proposal based on its Model 345 and the submission earned an order for three prototypes to be built under the designation XB-29. The first made its maiden flight in September 1942.

The Superfortress embodied many entirely new features, including the remarkable Boeing Model 117 wing design that greatly increased efficiency and performance. Computers were introduced in the form of the Superfortress' remote control gun-aiming system. There was also the innovative "three bubble" system of pressurization for the crew spaces. The pilots' cabin and the waist gunner's compartments were pressurized and connected by a pressurized tunnel. The tail gunner's area was pressurized independently. Pressurization allowed the B-29 to operate at much higher altitudes than previous bombers—such as the B-17—which were not pressurized.

The Superfortress featured not only unprecedented technology but unprecedented production challenges. To meet tight wartime deadlines, there were many bugs to be wrung out and wrung out quickly, not the least of which were with the new 2,200-horsepower Wright R3350-13 engines, a malfunction of which resulted in the loss of the second prototype and its crew.

Inspecting the huge B. F. Goodrich tires installed in a B-24 Liberator at the Ford Motor Company factory in Willow Run. *Howard Hollem, Office of War Information*

Nevertheless, the USAAF had committed to an initial order for 1,644 examples of the huge bomber before it had even entered its flight test phase of development. As was the case with both the B-17 and B-24, it was planned that the Superfortress would be manufactured at multiple locations. In fact, four brand-new factories were built even as the first prototypes were being tested. Boeing had built the three XB-29 prototypes in Seattle, but in order not to interfere with ongoing B-17 production there, the company built two facilities of its own. One was just a few minutes' flying time from Boeing Field at Renton, Washington. The other was at Wichita, Kansas, where Boeing already operated the former Stearman facilities, building Kaydett trainers.

While Boeing operated these two factories, Buffalo-based Bell Aircraft built a new Superfortress factory near Atlanta, Georgia, and the Baltimore-based Glenn Martin Company built a new facility at Omaha, Nebraska. Boeing built 1,620 B-29-BWs at Wichita, Bell produced 357

At work inside the fuselage of a
Consolidated-Vultee B-24 Liberator.
Author collection

B-29-BAs in Atlanta, and Martin built 204 B-29-MOs in Omaha. In addition, 1,119 B-29A-BNs would be built by Boeing at Renton and 310 B-29B-BAs would be built in Atlanta by Bell.

When the Superfortress fleet was ready for combat in mid-1944, the USAAF had decided to concentrate the entire force against Japan rather than to use some against Germany. USAAF commander General Henry H. "Hap" Arnold even set up an all-new Air Force, the Twentieth, to manage the B-29 armada. Although the momentum of World War II had shifted in 1943, it was in 1944 that the Allies were able to amass sufficient numbers of troops and equipment to finally crush the Axis. In the Pacific, 1943 was a year of holding actions, but in 1944 the Allies launched a series of major offensives aimed at retaking Japanese-held islands. Guam and the Mariana Islands were recaptured in August, giving Hap Arnold the bases he needed to conduct his decisive B-29 offensive against Japan.

Across the globe, the Allies were bringing the war home to Hitler's Third Reich. Thanks in large part to all the factories in the United States that were turning out thousands upon thousands of B-17s and B-24s, Allied bombers undertook a wide-ranging strategic bombing offensive aimed at destroying the German railroad network and industrial infrastructure.

The largest military operation of 1944, and indeed of the entire war, was Operation Overlord, the Allied invasion of northern France on June 6. Nearly 3 million Allied troops, 5,000 ships, and more than 15,000 aircraft took part in crossing the English Channel to the Normandy coast. On August 25, the Allies marched triumphantly into Paris.

The American aircraft industry had reached its zenith during the first half of 1944, employing more people and delivering more aircraft than had ever been delivered at any time before or since by any aircraft industry anywhere. More than 81 production plants in the United States, comprising 175 million square feet, plus another five American-owned or operated factories in Canada, hummed in a symphony of production. A workforce of more than 2.1 million men and women built airframes, engines, and propellers. The value of the industry had risen incredibly, from $225 million in 1939 (approximately $3.2 billion in current dollars) to $16 billion (approximately $178 billion in current dollars) in 1944. During 1944, the American aircraft industry built an incredible 96,318 aircraft, up 12 percent from the year before.

In the United Kingdom, aircraft production fell in 1944 for the first time since the depths of the Great Depression, dropping 6 percent to 24,461 units. In the Soviet Union, there was a 14 percent increase to about 40,300 aircraft.

During 1944, Germany launched an unprecedented industrial mobilization of its own, increasing its annual aircraft output half again to about 40,000. However, while American workers were doing their unprecedented work for unprecedented salaries, German industry was accomplishing its production increase with slave labor.

At work in a wing section of the huge Boeing B-29 Superfortress at Renton in 1944. *Boeing Archives*

By the last quarter of 1944, the heavy bombers that streamed out of factories from the Southland to Texas and from Seattle to Willow Run, had so decimated German infrastructure that it was just weeks away from total collapse. Japan, too, increased aircraft production in 1944, to 28,180 units. However, as in Germany, draconian slave labor propped up an industry on the verge of implosion.

With Axis industry on the brink, the entire United States industrial plant was creating a production miracle. The January 10, 1944, issue of *Time* magazine reported that, since 1940, "Aircraft plant equipment had increased 40 times. Aluminum capacity had increased sevenfold. Steel capacity had increased 15 percent—in an industry that had operated for six out of ten prewar years at half capacity or less. Machine tools had been produced in three times the volume of all ten prewar years put together."

Indeed, the industrial mobilization of the United States economy for World War II had wrested the nation from the grip of the Great Depression. As Alan Milward wrote in *War, Economy and Society*, "War

B-29 Superfortress bombers near completion on the floor of Boeing's big new factory in Renton, Washington, in late 1944. *Boeing Archives*

Lillian Salstrom works on one of the big pressurized bulkheads within a B-29 Superfortress at Renton, Washington, in December 1944. She is sitting on the aircraft's floor. A pressurized tube that connected the aft gun positions with the flight deck ran through the circular opening at the top. *Boeing Archives*

B-29 Superfortress bombers near completion on the floor of Boeing's big new factory in Renton, Washington, in late 1944. *Boeing Archives*

demands and the preparations for war were the real force bringing the United States economy out of prolonged depression; the period from 1940 to 1944 witnessed the largest expansion in industrial production in United States history. The switch from butter to guns was clearly depicted by the enormous shift in the composition of America's income: War production in 1939 was 2 percent of total output, in 1941 10 percent and in 1943 40 percent."

Harold Vatter further pointed out in *The US Economy in World War II* that the high unemployment and low-capacity utilization of the Great Depression meant that the United States economy had essentially started

from next to nowhere in 1940 and that "almost all the war output came from the increase in GNP."

For the American aircraft industry, the peak production month of all time was March 1944, with more than 9,000 aircraft coming off the assembly lines. By this time, the industry had outdone itself, producing more aircraft than the armed forces of the United States and its Allies could absorb. By the second quarter of 1944, production had to be deliberately decreased.

The U.S. Army Air Forces took delivery of a wartime high 14,822 aircraft in the first quarter of 1944, but the second quarter total of

ABOVE: The Glenn L. Martin facility in Omaha, Nebraska, was one of several brand-new factories to be built in record time during World War II in order to turn out large numbers of B-29 Superfortresses. *Glen L. Martin Company*

RIGHT: A huge armada of B-29 Superfortress "Very Heavy" bombers moves rapidly toward completion in 1944. *Boeing archives*

RIGHT: These two technicians at the Boeing plant in Wichita, Kansas, work inside what will be the pressurized tube connecting the aft crew sections to the flight deck of a B-29 Superfortress. *Boeing Archives*

OPPOSITE: The wing section of a B-29 Superfortress "flies" in to mate with the center fuselage section. *Boeing Archives*

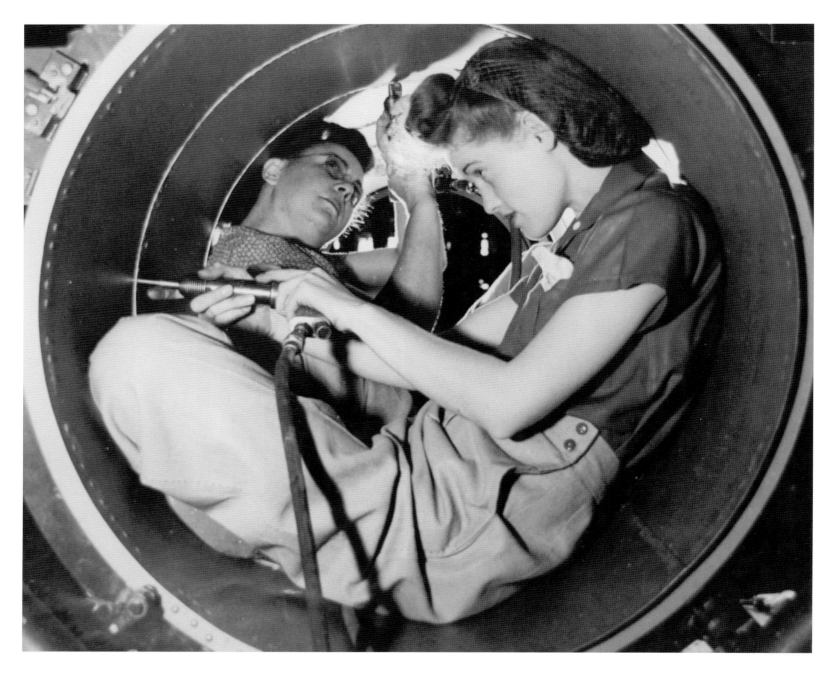

13,782 was still higher than any quarter during 1943. Even with its throttle pulled back, the mighty engine of the American aircraft industry was still roaring with incredible velocity.

The USAAF would receive 51,547 aircraft during 1944, compared to 45,889 in 1943. In both years, these totals represented only 53 percent of the total number of aircraft built by the American aircraft industry. Of the USAAF total in 1944, 35 percent were fighters, 25 percent were heavy bombers, 11 percent were transports, 8 percent were trainers, and 7 percent were medium bombers. By comparison, in 1942, 19 percent were fighters, 7 percent were heavy bombers, 4 percent were transports, 9 percent were medium bombers, and almost half were trainers. By 1944, the services had about enough training aircraft on hand to train the pilots that were necessary to win the war.

In terms of both personnel and hardware, the American aircraft industry was a very well oiled mechanism in the arsenal of democracy that was the United States.

Chapter Five

Toward Victory and Beyond

B y the end of 1944, Germany and Japan had lost control of most of the territory they had conquered earlier in World War II. Although they had no hope of winning, they desperately continued to fight on, making the final Allied victory a very costly one for all sides—but especially so for Germany and Japan. Earlier in the war, great battles had raged for mastery of the airspace of global battlefronts, but by the end of 1944, U.S. forces controlled the skies above every global battlefront where American surface forces fought, and American bombers were conducting devastating raids into the Axis heartland.

When U.S. armed forces entered World War II with a desperate need for military aircraft, the American aircraft industry responded with incredible vigor, its factories running day and night to meet the challenge. In May 1940, President Franklin Roosevelt startled the world by calling for 50,000 military aircraft. Between July 1940 and August 1945, the American aircraft industry would deliver 295,959, including 158,880 to the USAAF, and 73,711 to the U.S. Navy.

Four single factories exceeded 16,000 aircraft during World War II: the North American Aviation facilities at Inglewood, California, and Dallas; the flagship Curtiss plant at Buffalo; and the Grumman Iron Works on Long Island. According to official USAAF data, these four alone built more than 70,000 airplanes.

At the end of 1944, as the nation noted the third anniversary of Pearl Harbor, the USAAF was faced with the curious dilemma of having

more aircraft than it needed. On the eve of World War II, 2,230 aircraft for the U.S. Army Air Corps were seen as a "minimum safe peacetime strength," and a law setting this figure as a maximum rather than a minimum was in effect. In August 1944, the USAAF, successor to the U.S. Army Air Corps, reached it peak inventory of 79,660. Thereafter, older types, including trainers, were phased out of the inventory. The USAAF also had more pilots than it needed. In 1942, 42 percent of the aircraft delivered to the USAAF were trainers. In 1944, the percentage had dropped to just 9 percent.

At the same time, production of highly advanced aircraft was increasing rapidly. In all of 1943, the USAAF received fewer than 100 B-29 Superfortresses, but in just the second quarter of 1945, more than a thousand were delivered. Had the war not ended when it did, that number would have more than doubled in the third quarter. Aircraft

A large group of Block 80 Douglas C-47A Skytrain transports marches toward victory. The sign says that the assembly line moves at 9:00, but doesn't specify p.m. or a.m. It could have been either—the American aircraft industry was running 24 hours a day. *Courtesy Harry Gann*

LEFT: Powered turrets are built at the Glenn Martin Company. Note that the one in the foreground has been marked as "ready to fire." *Glenn L. Martin Company*

OPPOSITE: The payroll at the Glenn Martin Company plant in Omaha, Nebraska, was a cast of thousands. Though the huge B-29 Superfortresses were a high-visibility product, Martin built nearly three times as many B-26 Marauders here. *Glenn L. Martin Company*

such as the B-29 were winning the war. In October 1944, the Mariana Island chain—Guam, Saipan, and Tinian—was recaptured from the Japanese. The Twentieth Air Force was promptly relocated to bases in the Marianas, where they were closer to Japan and could be more easily resupplied. Through the winter, the number of available B-29s grew rapidly, and so did the intensity of the attacks on Japan. The number of B-29s available for a single mission grew from 200 to 400 to 600. On August 1, 1945, 784 Superfortresses reached their targets.

In Europe, the USAAF heavy bombers striking targets within Hitler's Third Reich routinely numbered more than a thousand on a given day. Between the USAAF Eighth Air Force in England and the USAAF Fifteenth Air Force in Italy, it was not uncommon for 2,000 heavy bombers to slam the Reich daily.

During the war, the American aircraft industry had become the world's largest single industry. As previously noted, according to the Civil Aeronautic Administration *Statistical Handbook*, America's

RIGHT: When World War II began some of the factories of the American aircraft industry still had cloth-covered biplanes on the floor. By the spring of 1945, Lockheed had a river of gleaming new P-80 Shooting Star jet fighters pouring off the line. *Lockheed California Company*

OPPOSITE: A Douglas Aircraft Company technician checks the tubing inside a wheel well of a bomber. *Courtesy Harry Gann*

aircraft factories produced 324,750 aircraft between 1939 and 1945, including 304,139 military aircraft. During 1942, the first full year of the United States' involvement in World War II, the American aircraft industry built 47,836 military aircraft. Two years later, at its peak, the industry built 96,318. First quarter deliveries to the U.S. Army Air Corps (USAAF after 1941) increased from 1,105 in 1941, to 5,537 in 1942, to 9,693 in 1943, and to 14,822 in 1944.

The government factory expansion program conducted between 1940 and 1943 saw the number of airframe, engine, and propeller factories in the United States double to more than 80. The newer factories were also much larger. Under the expansion program, the total floor space devoted to aircraft production increased from 13 million square feet in the prewar period to more than 167 million square feet in 1943.

Quantities of Aircraft Built for U.S. Armed Forces by Major Manufacturers

July 1940 through August 1945

Manufacturer	USAAF	U.S. Navy/USMC
North American	1,839	0
Douglas	25,569	5,411
Consolidated-Vultee	27,634	3,296
Curtiss	19,703	6,934
Lockheed	17,148	1,929
Boeing	17,231	291
Grumman	0	17,448
Republic	15,663	0
Eastern (GM)	0	13,449
Bell	12,941	1
Martin	7,711	1,272
Chance Vought	0	7,896
Beech	7,430	0
Ford	6,792	0
Fairchild	6,080	300
Piper	5,611	330
Cessna	5,359	0
Goodyear	0	3,940
Taylor	1,940	0

Source: *USAAF Statistical Digest*, 1945

The government policy of decentralizing the American aircraft industry had also worked, bringing employment to areas that had been ignored by the industry before the war. Nearly 90 percent of airframe manufacturing capacity measured in square feet of floor space was located in five states in 1940. By 1944, 12 states shared 85 percent of airframe floor space, and California had dropped from more than a third to 24 percent of the total.

As World War II came to its triumphant close in Tokyo Bay, the planemakers of the American aircraft industry took stock of what they had accomplished and began the task of reconverting to the postwar economy.

Curtiss-Wright, the inheritor of the two oldest dynasties in American aviation, had built 17,489 aircraft during World War II at its

ABOVE: A crane at the Douglas Aircraft Company unloads a forward fuselage section for a Douglas transport. During the war, Douglas became the leader in American military transports. Its ubiquitous C-47 was produced in the largest numbers, and its C-54 became the standard four-engine, long-range transport. *Courtesy Harry Gann*

OPPOSITE: A-26 Invader attack bombers on the assembly line near the end of the war. Douglas produced Invaders in both Tulsa, Oklahoma, and Long Beach, California. Though production ended abruptly at the two locations in August and September 1945, respectively, Invaders continued in service for a generation. *Courtesy Harry Gann*

Quantities of Aircraft Built for U.S. Armed Forces by Major Manufacturers

July 1940 through August 1945

Company and Location	Number Produced
North American (Dallas, TX)	18,784
Curtiss-Wright (Buffalo, NY)	17,489
Grumman Aircraft (Bethpage, NY)	17,478
Lockheed (Burbank, CA)	17,148*
North American (Inglewood, CA)	16,447
Bell Aircraft (Buffalo, NY)	12,941
Consolidated-Vultee (Downey, CA)	11,687
Boeing (Wichita, KS)	9,890
Douglas (Long Beach, CA)	9,439

* Lockheed operated the two Burbank plants separately.

Source: *USAAF Statistical Digest*, 1945

The Most Productive U.S. Aircraft Engine Factories

July 1940 through August 1945

Company and Location	Number Produced
Pratt & Whitney (East Hartford, CT)	122,302
Wright Aeronautical (Paterson, NJ)	77,554
Buick (Flint, MI)	74,198
Allison (Indianapolis, IN)	69,305
Studebaker (South Bend, IN)	63,789
Wright Aeronautical (Lockland, OH)	61,940
Chevrolet (Tonowanda, NY)	60,766
Ford (Dearborn, MI)	57,178
Packard (Detroit, MI)	54,714

Source: *USAAF Statistical Digest*, 1945

flagship plant in Buffalo, 70 percent of that total in the P-40 Warhawk family. They also built 6,343 aircraft for the U.S. Navy at the Columbus, Ohio, plant that they built in 1941, and another 2,261 aircraft in St. Louis and 458 in Louisville, Kentucky.

Wright Aeronautical, the Curtiss-Wright engine division, built 77,554 of its Cyclone and Whirlwind radial engines in Paterson, New Jersey, and 61,940 in Lockland, Ohio. Licensed production of Wright engines—including 63,789 Cyclones built by Studebaker in South Bend, Indiana—brought the total number of wartime-built Wright radials to 223,036.

Pratt & Whitney was the single top producer of American aircraft engines during World War II, manufacturing 122,302 of its Wasp family of radials at its flagship plant in East Hartford, Connecticut,

ABOVE: A riveting team at work on the cockpit shell of a C-47 transport aircraft. Plexiglas panels would come later.
Alfred Palmer, Office of War Information

OPPOSITE: Douglas Aircraft inspectors at Long Beach, California, check and catalog inner wing sections of transport aircraft prior to their attachment to fuselage sections during final assembly.
Alfred Palmer, Office of War Information

Percentage of Total Airframe Weight Delivered by Major U.S. Manufacturers

July 1940 through August 1945

Manufacturer	Percent
Douglas	15.3
Consolidated-Vultee	14.6
Boeing	11.3
North American	10.5
Lockheed	9.0
Curtiss	6.9
Martin	6.3
Ford	6.2
Republic	6.9
Grumman	3.7
Bell	2.7
Eastern	2.4
Chance Vought	1.4
Goodyear	0.7
All others	2.1
Total	100.0

Source: *USAAF Statistical Digest*, 1945

and another 7,815 at its expansion facility in Kansas City. Having cited Pratt & Whitney as the single top producer, it should be added that the various autonomous divisions of General Motors, if counted together, produced 204,269. Clearly, however, engines of Pratt & Whitney design led the way. The total number of Wasp-family radial engines produced by Pratt & Whitney and its licensees reached 355,985 during the war, and more were built after the war.

Buick's Flint, Michigan, plant and Chevrolet's Tonowanda, New York, plant were the top two Pratt & Whitney licensees, producing 74,198 and 60,766, respectively. The Ford Motor Company built another 57,178 R2800 Double Wasps in Dearborn.

The General Motors Allison Division was the leading American maker of water-cooled inline aircraft engines during World War II, producing 69,305 in Indianapolis. Packard was in second place, building 54,714 Merlins in Detroit under license from Rolls-Royce.

(Allison became a subsidiary of Rolls-Royce in 1995, a half century after World War II.)

Other leading inline producers included Continental, which produced 29,625 (as well as 5,100 radials) in Muskegon, Michigan, and Lycoming, which manufactured 24,871 in Williamsport, Pennsylvania.

At its flagship factory in Middle River, near Baltimore, Maryland, the Glenn Martin Company produced 5,611 aircraft during World War II, of which two-thirds were B-26 Marauder medium bombers. The Martin expansion plant at Omaha, Nebraska, built 2,100 aircraft, including B-26s and Boeing-designed B-29s.

One of the most far-reaching turns of event to occur at Lockheed's Burbank campus during World War II occurred in complete secrecy and affected both the company and aviation history for the remainder of the twentieth century. In 1943 the USAAF selected Lockheed to build

continued on page 176

ABOVE: The wiring laid out on the plywood in the background served as a guide for technicians wiring P-51 Mustangs at North American Aviation. *Courtesy Earl Blount*

OPPOSITE: An electrician at the Douglas Aircraft Company prepares wiring to be incorporated into a warplane. *Courtesy Harry Gann*

RIGHT: Douglas technicians conduct the precise installation of a Pratt & Whitney R1830 Twin Wasp radial engine in a C-47 at the Long Beach plant. *Alfred Palmer, Office of War Information*

OPPOSITE: North American B-25 Mitchell bombers on the floor at the company's factory in Kansas City. USAAF records recall that North American built 6,608 of the bombers here. *Alfred Palmer, Office of War Information*

ABOVE: Assembling a section of the leading edge for the horizontal stabilizer of an aircraft in the North American Aviation Control Surface Department. *Alfred Palmer, Office of War Information*

RIGHT: Oxygen flask racks are installed above the flight deck of a C-87 transport at the Consolidated-Vultee plant in Fort Worth, Texas. *Howard Hollem, Office of War Information*

continued from page 173

what was to be America's first *operational* jet fighter. (The first USAAF jet fighter, the Bell P-59, never reached squadron service.)

Kelly Johnson, the company's chief research engineer and the genius behind the P-38 Lightning, handpicked a team to turn highly experimental technology into a jet aircraft for mass production. Johnson's team was virtually sealed into a canvas-roofed building next to the Lockheed wind tunnel and told to design and build a prototype in 180 days—they accomplished the task in 143 days.

This was the beginning of the Lockheed Advanced Development Projects (ADP) office, which continues to be known, because of the conditions in its original home, as the Skunk Works. The name was

taken from the place where Al Capp's cartoon character, Li'l Abner, then popular on newspaper funny pages, distilled his "Kickapoo Joy Juice."

The prototype XP-80 Shooting Star that Johnson's Skunk Works created in record time made its first flight in January 1944 and became the first American fighter to exceed 500 miles per hour. The USAAF was delighted. Orders were issued, with plans for Lockheed to build 4,000 P-80As, and for North American Aviation to produce another 1,000 at their huge Dallas factory.

The Douglas Aircraft Company wrapped up its contribution to the war effort having built 25,569 aircraft for the USAAF and 5,411 for the U.S. Navy. This placed Douglas second only to North American Aviation as the largest producer in the American aircraft industry during World War II. The largest Douglas operation was the huge new plant at Long Beach that accounted for a third of the company's output during the war, including 4,285 C-47s. A quarter of the total—including 6,006 A-20s—came from the flagship plant in Santa Monica. All of the U.S.

Checking a drawing in the Drafting Department at Consolidated-Vultee.
Author collection

A clerk in a stockroom at North American Aviation in Inglewood, California, checks to see that the proper numbers of parts were received and placed in the proper bins. *Alfred Palmer, Office of War Information*

Navy work was done at El Segundo. Outside California, Douglas built 629 C-54s in Chicago during the war and 5,319 C-47 family transports at the new Oklahoma City facility. At Tulsa, Douglas ended the war having built 2,870 aircraft, including 1,291 A-26 Invaders.

Up the road from Long Beach at Inglewood, North American Aviation was the largest producer of American aircraft by a large margin, producing 41,839 during World War II. North American also had the distinction of producing the USAAF's most important

trainer, the AT-6/SNJ Texan family; its most important medium bomber, the B-25 Mitchell; and its most important fighter, the P-51 Mustang. The flagship plant at Inglewood produced 16,447 aircraft during the war, including 9,949 P-51s and 3,208 B-25s. The new Dallas facility was the company's top producer, with 18,784 aircraft, including 12,967 Texans, 4,552 Mustangs, and 966 Consolidated B-24s. The company's Kansas City operation, meanwhile, rolled out an impressive 6,608 Mitchells.

A blue shirt with the Vultee logo was standard company attire for employees at Vultee's Nashville facility. *Alfred Palmer, Office of War Information*

Boeing ended World War II as the world leader in four-engine-aircraft development. Its B-29 Superfortress was perceived as perhaps the most advanced piston-engine aircraft produced through the end of World War II. Boeing built 6,981 B-17s at its flagship plant in Seattle and 2,739 operational B-29 and B-29A bombers at its new factories at Renton and Wichita. The drawing boards at Boeing Field were already filled with designs for large jet bombers, a field that Boeing would dominate for a generation with its B-47 and B-52.

The company had also rolled out the initial examples of its C-97 Stratofreighter, a military transport with B-29 wings and tail. This would serve as the prototype aircraft for two of Boeing's major postwar products: the Stratocruiser airliner and the KC-97, the first airplane specifically factory-built in large numbers as an aerial refueling aircraft.

By war's end, Consolidated-Vultee had produced 30,930 aircraft, placing it just 500 units behind Douglas and in third place in the industry. The Vultee plant at Downey, California, led the way among the

The end of an era is marked by the last Consolidated-Vultee B-24M making its way down the San Diego assembly line in June 1945, the same month that the USAAF terminated all Liberator contracts. Behind it, for the first time in years, there are no more aircraft. The first B-24Ms had been delivered in October 1944 and this was the last of more than 900 built in San Diego. Within a few years, this line would be filled with commercial ConvairLiners. *Author collection*

Forward fuselage sections of B-29 Superfortress bombers on the floor at Boeing's big new factory in Renton, Washington, on June 14, 1945. Although B-24 contracts were cancelled in June 1945, the B-29 was in its ascendancy. Even after the war, there was still a modicum of demand for the state-of-the-art Superfortress. *Boeing Archives*

At work inside the fuselage of a B-29 Superfortress. The pressurized tube at the top permitted crew access between the flight deck area and the aft crew sections. Airmen prone to claustrophobia tended to stay put. *Boeing Archives*

company's factories, building 11,687 aircraft, mainly Valiant trainers. Vultee also built 1,966 aircraft at their expansion facility in Nashville, mostly Vengeance attack bombers. As a relic of a 1940 acquisition made by Avco, Vultee also operated the former Stinson factory in Wayne, Michigan, where 4,104 aircraft were built during World War II, mainly L-5 Sentinel light utility planes.

The Consolidated headquarters plant in San Diego produced 6,729 units, according to USAAF records, mainly the big four-engine B-24 Liberator heavy bombers. Consolidated also built 221 U.S. Navy patrol bombers in New Orleans and operated the vast USAAF Plant 4 facility north of Fort Worth. Built expressly for B-24 production, Fort Worth delivered 2,743 of them by war's end, along with 291 C-87 Liberator Expresses, the transport version of the big aircraft. Another product of the Fort Worth plant was the B-32 Dominator, a sort of "Super Liberator" ordered by the USAAF as a companion to the Boeing B-29. Originally known as the "Terminator," the first prototype XB-32 made its initial flight in 1942, and the first production B-32s were delivered late in 1944.

continued on page 188

ABOVE: A completed B-29 Superfortress rolls out of the Boeing Wichita factory and into the warm Kansas air. Boeing built 1,620 B-29s at Wichita during World War II. After the war, the factory was used for Boeing's B-47 and B-52 jet bombers. *Boeing Archives*

OPPOSITE: Looking futuristic are these large bulkheads that will be incorporated into the forward sections of B-29 Superfortresses. *Boeing Archives*

continued from page 185

Consolidated built 114 Dominators before the war ended and a few saw service in the Pacific, but the USAAF decided to concentrate production on the B-29, and the program was canceled in September 1945.

Throughout World War II, Consolidated engineers had been working on the largest piston-engine bomber that would ever be built. Though the B-36 Peacemaker did not make its debut flight until after the war, production of the huge aircraft kept the Fort Worth assembly line busy until 1955. In 1954, Convair became the Convair Division of General Dynamics Corporation and the Fort Worth plant was later used for production of the Convair B-58 and the General Dynamics F-111 and F-16. The F-16 program was sold to Lockheed in 1993. The latter company, which merged with Martin in 1994, continued to use the huge factory for F-16 production into the twenty-first century.

The Fort Worth factory is one of just a handful of the great aircraft factories built during World War II that survived past the turn of the century. Most of the vast archipelago of facilities that built 324,750 aircraft between 1939 and 1945 were gone by the end of the decade. Others closed during or between the major industry consolidations of the 1960s and 1990s. In addition to Fort Worth, another notable survivor was the Boeing plant at Renton, which started as a B-29 factory and became the site of the long-running production of 727, 737, and 757 commercial jetliners.

The years during World War II were a major turning point in aviation history. There has been no other six-year period in history when so many airplanes were manufactured, or so many pilots trained to fly. On a typical day in 1944, there were probably more airplanes in the air around the world than there are today, or than there have been on any day in any year in recent history.

In terms of production volume, the world will never see another year like 1944, when more than 225,000 airplanes were built in just five countries. In that same year, an even greater number of pilots earned their wings. The year that the United States entered World War II, the U.S. Army Air Forces had 150,000 personnel—by the beginning of 1944, there were 2.4 million people in USAAF uniforms, many of them pilots and aircrew members. At the beginning of the twenty-first century, the U.S. Air Force had just 356,000 personnel, of whom only 15 percent were pilots.

The U.S. Army Air Forces alone could field nearly 80,000 aircraft at the height of World War II, but the U.S. Air Force had only 6,800 aircraft at the time of the first Gulf War in 1991, a number that would be slashed by half within four years.

The story of the period from 1939 to 1945 is more than a story of numbers. In terms of aircraft technology, it was a story of monumental advances. In 1939, many of the aircraft in the world's air forces were still open-cockpit biplanes and monoplanes with ranges under 200 miles. It was almost as if time had stood still at the end of the previous world war. By the end of World War II, aircraft with pressurized flight decks were flying routine 5,000-mile missions in the stratosphere.

In 1939, one experimental jet aircraft had been tested for the first time and the technology was considered a novelty. By the autumn of 1944, jet fighter squadrons had become fully operational in Germany, and by the summer of 1945, the same was true for Britain and the United States. Dozens of types of jet aircraft that were on drawing boards in 1945 were in the air within three years. It was considered a milestone when an operational aircraft exceeded 400 miles per hour during World War II, but within a decade of the war's end, it was routine for aircraft to operate at supersonic speeds. Another decade after that, SR-71s were flying routinely at three times the speed of sound and at altitudes above 100,000 feet.

More than the raw numbers and the technology advances were the changes in the public's mood regarding themselves and their future. The phrase "the sky's the limit" became popular. People looked to the sky where so much had been accomplished and realized that the potential existed for so much more. A new generation stepped into and perpetuated a quarter-century boom of unprecedented promise and prosperity. This was a clear combination of both technology and the will and vision to use that technology.

In 1945, jet, rocket, and radar technology were combining to create new craft that in 1939 could not have been imagined by anyone outside the science fiction genre. Rockets were being prepared to probe the edge of space, to open mankind's vision and imagination to travel beyond Earth, and to land human beings on the moon less than 24 years after the guns fell silent.

The American aircraft factories themselves were a source of immense social change during World War II. Not only did they create jobs for 2.1 million Americans, they provided highly technical employment in places where such jobs were previously unavailable.

World War II saw women enter the American workforce in larger numbers than ever before. But nowhere in that greater industrial plant were they present in a larger proportion—or better paid—than in the American aircraft industry. The aircraft factories helped to create ethnic diversity and they played a role in altering the demographics of regions such as Southern California and western Washington state. Indeed, aircraft factories were responsible for these two West Coast regions becoming world leaders in aerospace technology and manufacture through the remainder of the century.

As Irving Brinton Holley so eloquently pointed out in the Center of Military History study *Buying Aircraft*, "A handful of major airframe builders received most of the publicity, but behind them lay the subcontractors and the suppliers or vendors, tier after tier, spreading out into every state in the union. Each firm, from the giant industrial complex to the tiny three-man back-yard job-shop turning out bits and pieces, played a significant role in the collective enterprise called aircraft production."

During World War II, the American aircraft industry had become the largest single industry in the United States, and the largest aircraft industry in the history of the world, before or since. In 1939, a total of 921 military aircraft were built in the United States. In 1944, the industry reached a peak annual production of 96,318. The statistics are staggering, the reasons are many, but first and foremost, it was America's aircraft workers who worked tirelessly, day and night for several long years, to make it happen. *Boeing Archives*

Bibliography

Books

Anderson, Fred. *Northrop: An Aeronautical History*. Northrop Corporation, 1976.

Anderton, David. *History of the U.S. Air Force*. Crescent, 1981.

Andrade, John M. *U.S. Military Aircraft Designations and Serials 1909 to 1979*. Midland Counties Publications, 1997.

Arnold, Henry Harley. *Global Mission*. Harper & Brothers, 1949.

Axe, E. W. *Aviation Industry in the United States*. Axe-Houghton Economic Studies, 1935–1938.

Blay, Roy. *Lockheed Horizons: A History of Lockheed*. Lockheed Aircraft Corporation, 1983.

Boeing Company. *Pedigree of Champions: Boeing since 1916*. The Boeing Company, 1985.

Bowers, Peter M. *Boeing Aircraft since 1916*. Aero Publishers, Naval Institute Press, 1966, 1989.

Christy, Joe. *The Illustrated Handbook of Aviation and Aerospace Facts*. Tab Books, 1984.

Civil Aeronautics Administration. *Statistical Handbook*. Civil Aeronautics Administration, 1948.

Corporate Publications. *Days of Trial and Triumph*. Lockheed Aircraft Corporation, 1969.

Craven, Wesley Frank and James Lea Cate. *Army Air Forces in World War II*. The University of Chicago Press, 1948.

————. *Men and Planes*. The University of Chicago Press, 1955.

Fahey, James C. *The Ships and Aircraft of the U.S. Fleet*. Ships and Aircraft, 1942–1946 (various editions).

————. *U.S. Army Aircraft 1908–1946*. Ships and Aircraft, 1946.

Fairchild, Byron and Jonathan Grossman. *The U.S. Army and Industrial Manpower*. US Army Center of Military History, 1959.

Francillon, Rene J. *Grumman Aircraft since 1929*. Naval Institute Press, 1989.

————. *Lockheed Aircraft since 1913*. Naval Institute Press, 1987.

————. *McDonnell Douglas Aircraft since 1920*. Naval Institute Press, 1988.

Green, William. *Famous Bombers of the Second World War*. Doubleday, 1957.

————. *Famous Fighters of the Second World War*. Doubleday, 1957.

————. *Warplanes of the Second World War*. Doubleday, 1964.

Harding, William Barclay. *The Aviation Industry*. C. D. Barney & Company, 1937.

Heinemann, Edward H. and Rosario Rausa. *Ed Heinemann: Combat Aircraft Designer*. Naval Institute Press, 1980.

Holley, Irving Brinton. *Buying Aircraft: Materiel Pocurement for the Army Air Forces*. U.S. Army Center of Military History, 1964.

Ingalls, Douglas J. *The Lockheed Story*. Aero Publishers, 1973.

————. *The McDonnell Douglas Story*. Aero Publishers, 1979.

Jane's. *All the World's Aircraft*. Jane's, 1938–1945 (annual editions).

————. *Jane's Fighting Aircraft of World War II*. Military Press, 1989.

Kelsey, Benjamin. *The Dragon's Teeth: The Creation of United States Air Power for World War II*. Smithsonian Institution Press, 1982.

Koistinen, Paul A. C. *Arsenal of World War II: The Political Economy of American Warfare, 1940–1945*. University Press of Kansas, 2004.

Lahm, Frank. *How Our Army Grew Wings*. Ronald Press, 1943.

Larkins, William T. *U.S. Marine Corps Aircraft 1914–1959*. Orion Books, 1988.

————. *U.S. Navy Aircraft 1921–1941*. Orion Books, 1988.

LeMay, General Curtis E. and Bill Yenne. *Superfortress: The B-29 and American Air Power in World War II*. McGraw-Hill, 1988; Westholme, 2006.

Lilley, Thomas. *Problems of Accelerating Aircraft Production during World War II*. Harvard University, 1947.

Long, S. Thomas. *The Undreamed-Of Marks: A Tribute to Jerry Vultee*. General Dynamics, 1991.

Maurer, Maurer. *Air Force Combat Units of World War II*. Office of Air Force History, 1983.

Milward, Alan S. *War, Economy and Society, 1939–1945*. University of California Press, 1977.

Seversky, Alexander de. *Victory through Air Power*. Simon & Schuster, 1942.

Smothers, Jack. *Convair Aerospace Division of General Dynamics Fiftieth Anniversary*. General Dynamics, 1973.

USAAF. *Army Air Forces Statistical Digest, World War II*. Director, Statistical Services, USAAF, 1945, 1945.

Vatter, Harold G. *The U.S. Economy in World War II*. Columbia University Press, 1985.

Wagner, Ray. *American Combat Planes, Third Enlarged Ed.* Doubleday, 1982.

Watson, Mark Skinner. *Chief of Staff: Prewar Plans and Preparations*. Historical Division, Department of the Army, 1950.

Wegg, John. *General Dynamics Aircraft and Their Predecessors*. Naval Institute Press, 1990.

Woods, James Bryant. *The Aircraft Manufacturing Industry*. White, Weld & Company, 1946.

WPA Writers' Program. *Who's Who in Aviation*. Ziff-Davis, 1938–1945 (annual editions).

Yenne, Bill. *Convair: Into the Sunset*. Greenwich/General Dynamics, 1995.

————. *The History of the U.S. Air Force*. Simon & Schuster, 1984; Hamlyn, 1992.

————. *Lockheed*. Random House/Photobook Information Service, 1987.

————. *McDonnell Douglas: A Tale of Two Giants*. Random House/Arms & Armour, 1985.

————. *Rockwell: The Heritage of North American*. Random House/Crescent, 1989.

————. *Secret Weapons of World War II*. Penguin Putnam, 2003.

————. *The Story of the Boeing Company*. AGS BookWorks/Zenith Press, 2005.

Yenne, Bill and Robert Redding. *Boeing: Planemaker to the World*. Crown/Random House, 1983; Arms & Armour, 1989.

Periodicals

Douglas Airview. Inclusive: 1939–1945.

Lockheed Horizons. Lockheed Aircraft Corporation, Lockheed-California Company. Inclusive: 1965-1995.

Los Angeles Times. January 2, 1943.

Marshall, J. W. *Iron Age*. "Line Production the Keynote of New Pratt and Whitney Aircraft Plant," July 17, 1930.

Saturday Evening Post. May 29, 1943.

Time Magazine. January 19, 1942; July 5, 1943; August 2, 1943; January 10, 1944.

Index